DISEASES & DISORDERS

Colon Cancer

Toney Allman

LUCENT BOOKS

A part of Gale, Cengage Learning

Detroit • New York • San Francisco • New Haven, Conn • Waterville, Maine • London

© 2012 Gale, Cengage Learning

LIBRARY OF CONGRESS CATALOGING-IN-PUBLICATION DATA

Allman, Toney.
  Colon cancer / by Toney Allman.
    p. cm. -- (Diseases and disorders)
  Summary: "This series objectively and thoughtfully explores topics of medical importance. Books include sections on a description of the disease or disorder and how it affects the body, as well as diagnosis and treatment of the condition"-- Provided by publisher.
  Includes bibliographical references and index.
  ISBN 978-1-4205-0792-8 (hardback)
  1. Colon (Anatomy)--Cancer--Popular works. I. Title.
  RC280.C6A42 2012
  616.99'4347--dc23

                        2012002941

Lucent Books
27500 Drake Rd.
Farmington Hills, MI 48331

ISBN-13: 978-1-4205-0792-8
ISBN-10: 1-4205-0792-3

Printed in the United States of America
1 2 3 4 5 6 7 16 15 14 13 12

Table of Contents

Foreword   4

Introduction
   A Scary Disease   6

Chapter One
   What Is Colon Cancer?   8

Chapter Two
   The Cause and Diagnosis of Colon Cancer   24

Chapter Three
   Treatment of Colon Cancer   39

Chapter Four
   Living with Colon Cancer   55

Chapter Five
   The Future of Colon Cancer   69

Notes   84

Glossary   90

Organizations to Contact   93

For More Information   95

Index   97

Picture Credits   103

About the Author   104

"The Most Difficult Puzzles Ever Devised"

Charles Best, one of the pioneers in the search for a cure for diabetes, once explained what it is about medical research that intrigued him so. "It's not just the gratification of knowing one is helping people," he confided, "although that probably is a more heroic and selfless motivation. Those feelings may enter in, but truly, what I find best is the feeling of going toe to toe with nature, of trying to solve the most difficult puzzles ever devised. The answers are there somewhere, those keys that will solve the puzzle and make the patient well. But how will those keys be found?"

Since the dawn of civilization, nothing has so puzzled people—and often frightened them, as well—as the onset of illness in a body or mind that had seemed healthy before. A seizure, the inability of a heart to pump, the sudden deterioration of muscle tone in a small child—being unable to reverse such conditions or even to understand why they occur was unspeakably frustrating to healers. Even before there were names for such conditions, even before they were understood at all, each was a reminder of how complex the human body was, and how vulnerable.

While our grappling with understanding diseases has been frustrating at times, it has also provided some of humankind's most heroic accomplishments. Alexander Fleming's accidental discovery in 1928 of a mold that could be turned into penicillin has resulted in the saving of untold millions of lives. The isolation of the enzyme insulin has reversed what was once a death sentence for anyone with diabetes. There have been great strides in combating conditions for which there is not yet a cure, too. Medicines can help AIDS patients live longer, diagnostic tools such as mammography and ultrasounds can help doctors find tumors while they are treatable, and laser surgery techniques have made the most intricate, minute operations routine.

This "toe-to-toe" competition with diseases and disorders is even more remarkable when seen in a historical continuum. An astonishing amount of progress has been made in a very short time. Just two hundred years ago, the existence of germs as a cause of some diseases was unknown. In fact, it was less than 150 years ago that a British surgeon named Joseph Lister had difficulty persuading his fellow doctors that washing their hands before delivering a baby might increase the chances of a healthy delivery (especially if they had just attended to a diseased patient)!

Each book in Lucent's Diseases and Disorders series explores a disease or disorder and the knowledge that has been accumulated (or discarded) by doctors through the years. Each book also examines the tools used for pinpointing a diagnosis, as well as the various means that are used to treat or cure a disease. Finally, new ideas are presented—techniques or medicines that may be on the horizon.

Frustration and disappointment are still part of medicine, for not every disease or condition can be cured or prevented. But the limitations of knowledge are being pushed outward constantly; the "most difficult puzzles ever devised" are finding challengers every day.

A Scary Disease

A diagnosis of cancer is frightening. A diagnosis of colon cancer can seem almost like a death sentence. In the past, as recently as the 1970s, half of all people who had colon cancer died within five years of being diagnosed. Today, however, the situation has changed. According to the National Cancer Institute of the National Institutes of Health, most people who get most kinds of cancer survive. Today, about 11 million Americans are cancer survivors, and colon cancer—especially when diagnosed early—is a treatable disease. Hayley Storrs, a British woman whose mother survived colon cancer, says, "Cancer does not have to be the end. . . . Cancer doesn't have to be such a scary word."[1]

In 2010 the National Cancer Institute issued a progress report on the United States' fight against cancer. In 1992 the U.S. death rate from cancer started to drop, and the number of new cases of cancer began to decline in 1999. In 2010 both the death rates and the rates of new cases of colon cancer continued along this decline. The death rate for colon cancer has fallen 40 percent since the 1970s. In addition, says the report, "Many people who have had cancer live longer and enjoy a better quality of life than was possible years ago."[2] Advances in diagnosis and improved treatment options have helped millions of people become colon cancer survivors.

Becoming a Survivor

Despite the progress made in diagnosing and treating colon cancer, it remains a serious disease that threatens the lives of those it affects. Many people still die from the disease, and for those who survive, recovery can take a long time and involve difficult, often uncomfortable procedures. Jen Puglise, for example, has been fighting colon cancer for four years and describes what is normal for her as "my life of surgeries, chemotherapy, doctor's appointments, and hospital stays."[3] Despite the challenges, Puglise says she is living her life to the fullest and is hoping for a cure someday.

Many people who have had colon cancer have already achieved the goal of being cancer free. Businessman and candidate for the 2012 Republican presidential nomination Herman Cain, for instance, was diagnosed with colon cancer in March 2006 and underwent nine months of treatment. In October 2011 Cain said, "Two months ago, I went to see my oncologist [cancer doctor] in Atlanta, got a full-scale check-up, CAT scan, X-rays, all of the various blood tests, and he put it in writing that, after five years, I am now totally, 100 percent cancer-free."[4] Cain's doctor, Luis Diaz, says that today Cain is probably "as normal and healthy as someone who doesn't have cancer."[5] Because he has survived for five years without the cancer coming back, Cain is considered to be a cancer survivor. With modern colon cancer treatments, Cain and many others can look forward to a healthy future, even though they have colon cancer in their pasts. Colon cancer is not necessarily a death sentence anymore.

CHAPTER ONE

What Is Colon Cancer?

Anita Mitchell of Washington State was forty-one years old when she found out she had colon cancer. During the fall of 2004 Anita began to have symptoms of the disease, but she did not know that the symptoms were serious. She had some digestive upset and some abdominal pain. She had diarrhea almost every morning, and sometimes she saw some blood in her bowel movements. For a while she thought maybe the digestive problems were caused by her coffee drinking. When she asked her doctor about the blood, he suggested that she had hemorrhoids—enlarged anal veins that can occasionally bleed but are not dangerous. Anita was a mother of three children and busy with preparations for the Thanksgiving and Christmas holidays. She did her best to ignore her symptoms until one morning in January 2005. That morning, when she went to the bathroom, she saw a lot of blood. She was frightened about what could be wrong and thought about her father who had died of colon cancer when he was forty-five years old. When she went to the doctor for tests, she discovered that she, too, had cancer in her colon, and it had spread from her colon to other organs in her body. Anita's life was in danger.

Sam Whiting, an oncologist, or medical specialist in cancer treatment and prevention, led a team of doctors who used several different treatments in an effort to save Anita from her cancer. She received surgery, chemotherapy, radiation, and powerful cancer drugs over a period of more than a year. The treatments were often very difficult to tolerate because of unpleasant side effects, but they worked. When the treatments were completed, there were no signs of cancer anywhere in Mitchell's body. By 2008 Whiting was able to say, "Anita is now off of all cancer-directed therapy and is being followed carefully for cancer recurrence. She remains free of detectable disease."[6]

Anita knows that her cancer could come back, or recur, so she continues to be medically checked on a regular basis. However, she is optimistic about the future, and so are her doctors. Today, she is a colon cancer survivor, but she knows she is lucky. Cancer is a very serious disease, and some people do not win their battles against it.

What Is Cancer?

Cancer, according to the National Cancer Institute of the National Institutes of Health, is not one but many diseases, and there are more than one hundred types. All the types of cancer, however, are characterized by abnormal cells that divide and multiply without control. Cancers are usually named for the organ in which they first begin. So colon cancer is cancer that begins in the colon, where abnormal cells grow and invade normal body tissues. "All cancers," explains the National Cancer Institute, "begin in cells, the body's basic units of life."[7] Living bodies are made up of cells. Each cell is controlled by the nucleus in the center of the cell that acts like the cell's brain. Inside the nucleus is the deoxyribonucleic acid (DNA) that makes up the thousands of genes that are arranged along the twenty-three pairs of chromosomes in a human cell nucleus. All of the cell's activities are chemically directed by the nucleus, and each cell performs its function according to its DNA instructions. A major function of the DNA code is to ensure that cells grow and divide normally so as to produce more cells when necessary to keep the body healthy. Cells are also programmed to die or self-destruct when they become too old or damaged to function in a healthy way. This is called apoptosis.

Cancer cells are cells in which the process of apoptosis has gone awry. The National Cancer Institute explains, "The genetic

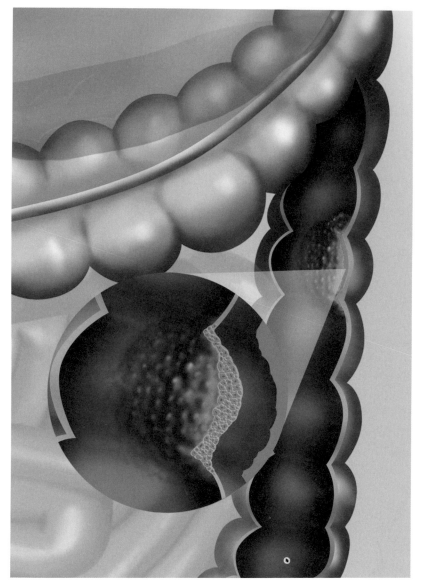

The inset shows cancer inside the colon.

material (DNA) of a cell can become damaged or changed, producing mutations that affect normal cell growth and division. When this happens, cells do not die when they should and new cells form when the body does not need them. The extra cells may form a mass of tissue called a tumor."[8] Mutations are changes in the DNA code that are permanent and that alter the genetic instructions for a cell's activity. In normal cell processes, this defective DNA is detected, and if it cannot be repaired, the cell receives chemical signals from the nucleus to self-destruct. At other times the body's immune system, which fights disease, detects and attacks the defective cell. In this way, many defective cells are destroyed by the body before they can cause any

A microscopic visualization of human chromosomes. Thousands of genes are arranged along twenty-three pairs of chromosomes in the nucleus of a human cell.

harm. In a cancer cell, however, the detection system did not work. The cell may divide uncontrollably and proliferate, or multiply, until it becomes a huge number of cells that invade and destroy normal tissues. These cells usually form a tumor, although sometimes cancer cells proliferate throughout the bloodstream, such as those that cause leukemia.

Whether or not cancer cells form tumors, they are referred to as malignant because they are able to destroy nearby tissue and to invade other parts of the body. Noncancerous tumors, known as benign tumors, can also form from abnormal cells, but they are not malignant, do not invade other tissues, and cannot spread to other parts of the body. Benign tumors are rarely life-threatening and usually can be removed from the body without incident. Colon cancer is a type of tumorous cancer called a carcinoma. Carcinomas are cancers that form in the skin or in the tissues that line internal organs.

What Is the Colon?

The colon is an internal organ that is part of the gastrointestinal (GI) tract. It is an essential part of the digestive system, and to understand how cancer affects the body it is important to understand how the GI tract works. The digestive system is the complex way that humans take in food, process the nutrients to make them usable by the body for energy and growth, and then eliminate the unusable waste from the body. The GI tract is essentially a series of organs connected by a long, winding tube that begins at the mouth and ends at the anus, where solid waste, or stool, is pushed out of the body. From the mouth, food is carried to the stomach, a very strong muscle that grinds the food and mixes it with acids and enzymes to break it down. Next, the mixture travels to the small intestine, or small bowel. Here, food is further broken down, and nutrients are absorbed into the bloodstream through the intestinal wall. Then, whatever is left over—the waste—is passed into the large intestine, or large bowel.

The colon and rectum are the two major parts of the large intestine. The colon is a muscular tube, about 5 to 7 feet (1.5

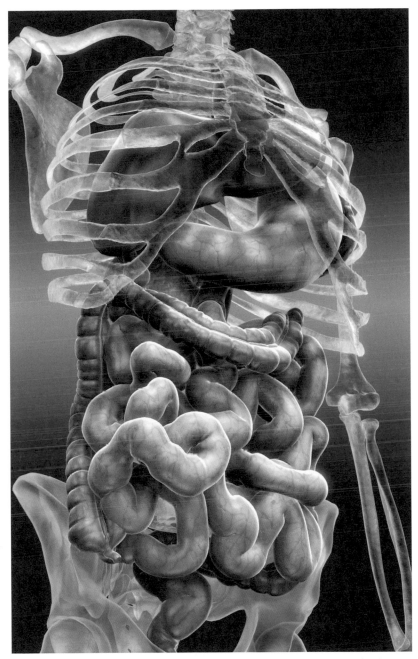

A close-up provides a view of a transparent skeleton with the gastrointestinal tract. The gastrointestinal tract is an essential part of the digestive system.

to 2.1m) long, that is made up of different parts that are named for their position in the abdominal cavity in the body. First is the cecum, which is a pouch that receives the waste from the small intestine in liquid form and passes it on to the ascending colon. The ascending colon is fixed in an upward position on the right side of the abdominal cavity. Here, the waste slowly travels through to the transverse colon, which lies horizontal across the abdominal cavity, and then through the descending colon, which extends down the left side of the abdominal cavity. As the muscles slowly push along the waste material through these segments of the colon, it extracts any extra water and minerals that can be absorbed and used by the body. This process makes the waste into a semisolid material. The semisolid waste is then pushed into the part of the colon called the sigmoid (S-shaped) colon, where it is stored until enough accumulates to be pushed into the rectum, where elimination begins. The rectum is a chamber about 8 inches (20.3cm) long. It receives the waste from the colon, sends signals to the brain that elimination is required, and then uses its muscles to hold the stool until the person decides to go to the bathroom. Then, it empties the contents through the anus. The anus is the last part of the GI tract.

Both the colon and rectum are made up of four layers of tissue. The innermost layer is called the mucosa. It is a membrane, somewhat like a thin skin, that produces mucus that lubricates and protects the inner walls of the colon and rectum. The layer of cells that lines the surface of the mucosa is called the epithelium. The next layer is the submucosa; it contains blood vessels and nerves. The third layer, the muscularis propria, is the muscle layer, and the fourth layer is the serosa, which is the membrane that encases the whole large intestine.

Cancer Cells in Polyps in the Colon

Colon cancer and rectal cancer almost always begin in the epithelium of the mucosa. Because these two parts of the large intestine are so similar in structure and in the way that cancer develops, many medical experts use the term colorectal cancer for cancers that develop in any part of the large intestine. Colorectal cancer arises in the rectum about 25 to 30 percent of the time, in the cecum about 15 to 20 percent of the time, in the sigmoid colon about 20 to 25 percent of the time, and in the ascending, transverse, or descending colon approximately 25 percent of the time. Usually, the cancer begins as a polyp on the epithelial layer of the colon or rectum.

A polyp is a small growth of tissue that forms on and protrudes from a mucous membrane. It is a benign (or noncancerous) lump of tissue, and most often, it does no harm. Several kinds of polyps can grow in the human body, but the kind called

An endoscopic view of a cancerous polyp inside an intestine. A polyp is a small growth of tissue that forms on and protrudes from a mucous membrane.

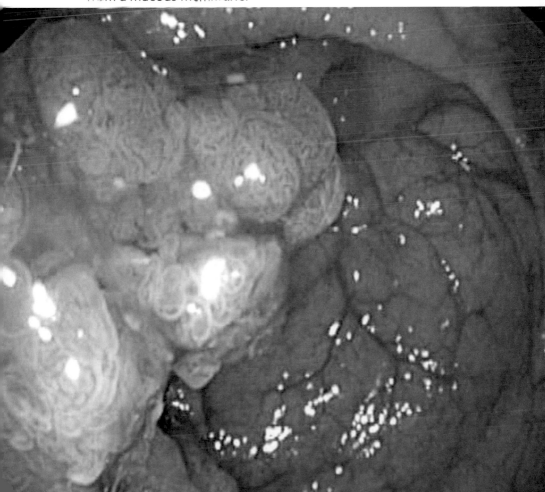

Possible Symptoms of Colon Cancer

Although many cases of colon cancer have no symptoms, the National Cancer Institute of the National Institutes of Health lists several possible symptoms that could be warning signs. These symptoms include having diarrhea or constipation, having a sensation of not being able to empty the bowel completely, finding blood in the bowel movement, having narrow bowel movements, experiencing cramps or a bloated feeling, losing weight without trying, feeling tired and fatigued, and having nausea or vomiting. None of these symptoms are unique to colon cancer. Many other digestive disorders can cause similar problems, but anyone experiencing these symptoms needs to be medically checked.

Possible symptoms of colon cancer include diarrhea, constipation, bloody bowel movements, and cramps or bloating.

an adenoma is the most likely to grow in the colon or rectum. The American Cancer Society explains about these polyps, "Adenomas start from a single cell and typically grow slowly, but over time they can grow to be larger than an inch. The risk of cancer within an adenoma increases as the size of the adenoma increases. Not all adenomas grow into cancer. In fact, fewer than 10 percent of adenomas become cancerous."[9] However, at least 95 percent of colorectal cancers begin with adenomas.

No one knows for sure why some adenomas become cancerous while most do not. The development of cancer is unpredictable. In addition, as an adenoma grows, it often causes no symptoms, and when cancer begins to develop in an adenoma, it may cause no symptoms either. A change in bowel habits (such as diarrhea, constipation, or gas and bloating) may be the only sign that something is wrong. Only when the polyp has grown to be about 0.7 inches (2cm) in size does it start to cause problems. At that point, it may bleed as the muscles of the large intestine try to push it out as if it were waste material. Cramps and diarrhea may be caused by this effort, too. The cancer in the adenoma grows slowly. The American Cancer Society says, "It is thought that the progression from normal epithelial cells to cancer takes, on average, 10 to 20 years."[10]

Cancer Cells Multiply and Spread

No matter how slowly it grows, if unchecked the cancer eventually spreads and extends through the inner lining of the colon or rectum and into the intestinal wall. If the tumor grows large enough, it can disrupt the normal functioning of the large intestine, damage tissues, and cause serious problems with elimination of stool, a blockage in the intestine, or a life-threatening tear in the colon. As the abnormal cells continue to divide and multiply, they can extend into the circulatory system (the bloodstream) where they are carried to other parts of the body. The cancer cells also may spread to nearby lymph nodes clustered in the abdomen. Lymph nodes are small nodules of tissue that are part of the lymphatic system, which is a major part of the body's immune system. Clear lymph fluid is transported by the lymphatic network from tissues to the bloodstream throughout the body. Once in the lymph nodes or the blood, it is easy for cancer cells to reach other body organs. The spread of cancer cells from the organ in which they originated to other organs is called metastasis. It is what happened to Anita Mitchell. The cancer that had started in her colon metastasized to other parts of her body, including her liver and several lymph nodes. When cancer has metastasized, it can form new tumors, damage other body organs, and eventually destroy their functioning. The longer cancer cells grow and spread, the more dangerous they are and the more likely they are to cause death.

Grades and Stages of Colon Cancer

As with all cancers, medical professionals describe colon or colorectal cancer by how aggressive it is, how extensive it is, and whether it has spread to other parts of the body. The aggressiveness of a cancer refers to how fast the cells are dividing and how different they look from normal cells under a microscope. Cancer cells are graded as 1 through 4, depending on the aggressiveness of the cancer, in a process called grading, or tumor grading. The higher the grade is, the less normal the cells appear. Often these cells are not well differentiated; unlike normal cells, a group of cancer cells may not have distinctive edges or structures or may not look like separate cells at all. The American Cancer Society explains, "A high grade means the cancer is more dangerous—that is, it is likely to grow fast and spread. For example, grade 1 (well-differentiated) cancers are the least aggressive, while grade 3 or 4 (poorly differentiated or undifferentiated) cancers are the most aggressive."[11]

To describe the extent of cancer and how far it has spread, medical professionals use a method called staging. The stage of colon cancer helps determine how life threatening the disease is and how it can be medically treated. Different systems may be used to describe the stages of cancer, but generally the stages are rated with Roman numerals 0 through IV, with IV

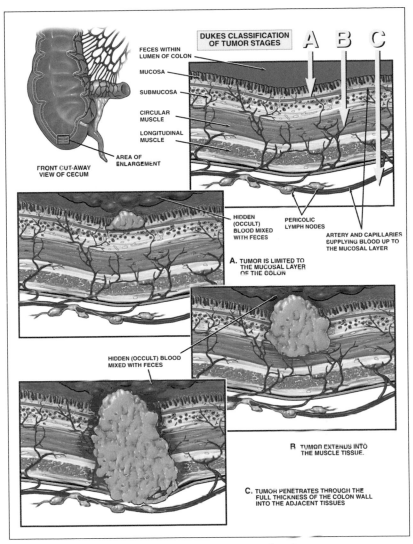

This illustration shows the various stages of colon cancer.

indicating the most severe cancer. Most medical profession-als assign the cancer to a particular stage on the basis of three important characteristics. This system, developed by American Joint Committee on Cancer, is called the TNM system. Accord-ing to the American Cancer Society, "T stands for the extent of the primary (main) colorectal tumor, N for the extent of lymph node involvement, and M for distant metastasis (spread) to other organs and tissues."[12] All three TNM elements are grouped together to determine the overall stage of the cancer. The stages of colon cancer are:

- Stage 0: The cancer is still in its earliest stage. The tumor is in the mucosa, the innermost layer of the colon, and has not spread anywhere.
- Stage I: The cancer cells have spread into the other layers of the colon but not yet to the outer wall.
- Stage IIA: The cancer has grown through the colon wall.
- Stage IIB: The cancer is through the wall and in nearby tissues but has not spread to any lymph nodes.
- Stage IIIA: The cancer is in the intestinal wall and has spread to one to three lymph nodes.
- Stage IIIB: The cancer has spread through the intestinal wall to nearby tissues *and* is in one to three lymph nodes.
- Stage IIIC: The cancer has metastasized and spread to four or more lymph nodes, but it has not spread to distant organs and tissues.
- Stage IV: The cancer has metastasized and has spread to other body organs, such as the liver or lungs.

The Danger of Colon Cancer

Mitchell's colon cancer, for example, was stage IV cancer. She had seven tumors on her liver and six affected lymph nodes. Stage IV cancer is the most severe, the most difficult to treat, and the hardest to survive. In 2011 the National Cancer Institute estimated that there were 141,210 new cases of colorectal cancer in the United States and 49,380 deaths from colorectal cancer in that year. Though the number of deaths is high, over the last twenty years death rates from colon cancer have fallen steadily. This decrease, reports the National Cancer Institute, is due to better health choices (such as less cigarette smoking), improved treatment methods, and improved cancer detection (catching the cancer in its early stages when it is easier to cure). Most of the colorectal deaths are in people with stage IV cancer, but individuals

Cancer of the Colon, Age-Adjusted SEER Incidence Rates, 2004–2008

Age at Diagnosis	All Races			Whites			Blacks		
	Both Sexes	Male	Female	Both Sexes	Male	Female	Both Sexes	Male	Female
All Ages	33.9	38.3	30.6	33.5	38.0	30.0	43.9	50.1	39.7
Under 65	11.5	12.7	10.4	11.0	12.2	9.8	16.8	18.3	15.6
65 and over	188.9	215.1	170.0	189.2	216.1	169.6	230.9	270.0	206.6
All ages (IARC world std)*	20.4	23.0	18.2	19.9	22.6	17.6	27.5	31.2	24.8

*Rates are per 100,000 and are age-adjusted to the IARC World Standard Population.

Taken from: http://seer.cancer.gov

like Mitchell are proof that people can and do survive even stage IV colon cancer.

Though colon cancer is the second leading cause of cancer deaths (after lung cancer) in the United States, not everyone will be affected by it, and not everyone is at the same risk of developing colon cancer. According to the National Cancer Institute, only about 5.1 percent of people born today will develop colorectal cancer at some time during their lives. The risk of developing colorectal cancer increases as people age, however. For example, less than 1 percent of colon cancer diagnoses are in people between the ages of 20 and 34. That percentage rises to 10.9 for people 45 to 54 years of age and to 28.8 in people between 75 and 84 years old. So, colon cancer is usually a disease of middle-aged people or the elderly. They are the ones at greatest risk for developing colon cancer, and the disease is uncommon in younger people. However, colon cancer can affect young people, too. Heidi, for example (full name withheld for privacy), was just thirty-one years old when she discovered that she had stage IV colon cancer in 1998. She says she was "well below the 'normal' age range," and adds, "I felt

Remission and Recurrence

When cancer treatment has been successful, and a person no longer shows any signs or symptoms, doctors do not immediately declare the person cured. Instead, they say that the person is in remission. Remission means that the signs and symptoms have gone away, and no cancer cells can be found in the person's body. Doctors know, however, that cancer is unpredictable and may return after a period of remission. Remission, therefore, is not the same as a cure. In general, doctors refer to a cure only after the cancer has been in remission for at least five years.

Recurrence is the term for cancer that returns after a period of remission—usually of a year or more. After five years of being cancer free, however, there is just a small chance that the cancer will return. Usually, say cancer experts, 80 percent of colon cancer recurrences happen within the first two years of remission. About 19 percent of recurrences happen within two to five years. Only 1 percent of recurrences happen after five years. The longer a person is in remission, the greater the chance that colon cancer will not recur.

like I was the only one of my age with colon cancer."[13] Heidi's experience was unusual, but she is not the only young person to develop colon cancer. Anyone can develop colorectal cancer, although the risk for young people is very low. Heidi, however, did succeed at becoming a survivor. Like Mitchell, she was cured of her cancer, despite its metastasis, and celebrated her eleventh year of cancer-free life in 2009.

A Survivable Disease

Today, the overall colorectal cancer survival rate (which is based on surviving for at least five years after the cancer is first diagnosed) is about 64.3 percent. However, when colon cancer is discovered and treated early, when it is still in stage I, the five-year survival rate is more than 90 percent. Any kind of cancer, at any stage, can be a frightening and dangerous disease, but colon cancer is survivable. Doctors and other medical professionals say that colon cancer is not only a treatable disease, but in most cases a preventable one, especially when the polyps that lead to colorectal cancer are identified before they can do any harm.

CHAPTER TWO

The Cause and Diagnosis of Colon Cancer

When Molly McMaster was diagnosed with stage II colon cancer, she was just twenty-three years old. Her first reaction was fear that she was going to die. "And," she thought, "how could this have happened to me anyway? I wasn't at risk. It didn't run in my family. I was a healthy twenty-three year old female, who worked out regularly, only had an occasional drink, didn't smoke or do drugs, and there I was with cancer."[14] Scientists still do not completely understand the cause of cancer, and they do not know, in all cases, why some people get cancer while others do not. They do not know exactly what goes wrong in the body that allows cancer to begin developing. Medical experts do know, however, that cancer begins with mistakes, or mutations, in genes. They know that multiple factors can put a person at greater risk of developing colon cancer. These risk factors do not predict colon cancer in any one individual, but they do indicate the people who should be medically followed, or checked and screened, so that a diagnosis can be made early and lives can be saved. Often, with the right diagnostic tests, colon cancer can even be prevented.

Genes and Cancer

The risk factors for developing cancer are both genetic and environmental. Genetic factors can be inherited—meaning that a person is born with one or more mutated genes—or genes can be damaged because of exposure to environmental factors or because mistakes are made as cells divide. When a cell divides, it has to make a copy of its DNA before splitting into two daughter cells. Mistakes made during the copying process are like typographical errors that change the coding instructions for that cell. Usually, these mistakes do no harm, but sometimes the mutations make it more likely that a cell will become cancerous.

Oncogenes are abnormal, mutated genes. They are genes in a cancer cell that influence the mutation, amplification, and proliferation of the cell.

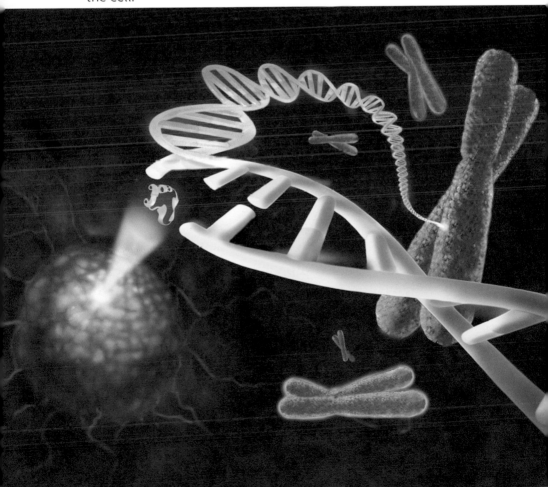

Modern medical researchers have learned that one mutated gene is usually not enough to cause cancer to develop. Generally, explains the nonprofit British organization Cancer Research UK, about half a dozen mutations must occur over time for a cell to become cancerous. Researchers have identified three different types of genes that are important in the development of cancer. The genes of one type instruct a cell to divide and multiply. Normally, these genes are most active when a person is still growing. In adults, these genes are not turned on and active unless a part of the body has been wounded or damaged and needs to be repaired. Abnormal, mutated genes, however, may instruct cells to multiply unnecessarily. These genes are called oncogenes, meaning cancer genes. Other kinds of genes, called tumor suppressor genes, instruct cells to stop multiplying. If these genes are damaged or turned off or missing, cells may multiply uncontrollably, also. The third type of genes that are involved in cancer growth are called DNA repair genes. Cancer Research UK says, "These genes normally repair any damage to the DNA that makes up the cell's genes. If these DNA repair genes are damaged, then other mutations are not repaired and the cell can copy the mutations into its daughter cells."[15] So, a cell may become cancerous because its genetic instructions direct it to multiply, fail to direct it to stop multiplying, or fail to instruct it to die when its DNA is damaged.

Genes and Colon Cancer

Scientists have been able to identify a few specific mutated genes that are inherited and may lead to the development of colon cancer. One kind of DNA repair gene, named by scientists HNPCC, is known to be involved in colon cancer in some people. A particular kind of mutation in this gene runs in families. Of the people who inherit the faulty HNPCC gene, 90 percent of men and 70 percent of women will develop colorectal cancer by age seventy. The mutated gene can also cause people to develop cancer at a young age. However, inheriting this mutated gene is rare. Researchers believe that only about 5 percent of colorectal cancer is caused by this mutated gene.

Dr. Oz Gets Screened

When he turned fifty years old in 2010, television personality and medical doctor Mehmet Oz decided to do a special segment on his show about colon cancer screening. He asked CBS medical correspondent Jonathan LaPook to perform a colonoscopy on him that was filmed for the *Dr. Oz Show*. Oz was just trying to set a good example for his viewers and publicize the importance of colon cancer screening, but he was in for a shock. LaPook found an adenoma during Oz's colonoscopy. LaPook was as surprised by the results as Oz was. Oz has none of the risk factors for colon cancer or polyps. He lives an extremely healthy lifestyle. He exercises, is not overweight, does not smoke, and eats a healthy diet. Neither colon cancer nor polyps run in his family. Both doctors say that the finding proves how essential screening is. Oz says about the whole experience, "The only thing holding me back from a terrible outcome is the dumb luck that I checked myself out for the show. I would have put this off, like a lot of people. But I bet this saved my life."

Quoted in Jonathan LaPook and Neil Katz. "Dr. Oz Cancer Scare: 'Dumb Luck . . . Saved My Life.'" Health Pop. CBS News, September 3, 2010. www.cbsnews.com /8301-504763_162-20015520-10391704.html.

When Dr. Oz had a colonoscopy on his TV show as part of a segment on colon cancer screening, the test revealed an adenoma even though he had no risk factors for colon cancer or polyps. The incident stressed the importance of screening.

Another inherited cause of colon cancer is called familial adenomatous polyposis (FAP). More than 95 percent of people
with this genetic syndrome will develop the polyps called
adenomas by the time they are in their thirties. Most of these
people eventually develop colon cancer. FAP is so rare, however, that it accounts for only 1 percent of all colon cancers.

About 20 percent of people who get colon cancer have a
close family member who has also had colon cancer, so researchers know that a family history of colon cancer is a risk
factor. All the genes that control this risk have not been identified, but scientists suspect that multiple genes may be involved
and passed down in families. However, most people in these
families do not develop colon cancer, and most people who
get colon cancer do not have family members who have colon
cancer. Even people who have genetic mutations known to be
linked to colon cancer do not get cancer 100 percent of the
time. While genes may increase risk, they are still only part of
the risk. Inherited genes may predispose an individual or make
him or her more vulnerable to developing colorectal cancer,
but clearly they are not the only cause of the disease.

The Environment and Carcinogens

Scientists theorize that even when colon cancer runs in families, the cause may not always be inherited gene mutations.
The staff of the Mayo Clinic says, "In some cases, this con-
nection may not be hereditary or genetic. Instead, cancers
within the same family may result from shared exposure to an
environmental carcinogen or from diet or lifestyle factors."[16] A
carcinogen is any substance in the environment that increases
the risk of developing cancer. It is a substance that damages a
cell's DNA. Usually, many changes in the DNA are necessary
before a cell becomes cancerous, and this means that over
time, as more and more DNA damage occurs, an individual
cell is more likely to become cancerous. Therefore, one of the
most important risk factors for developing cancer is age. Older
people are much more at risk of developing cancer than young
people because cells have had time to become more damaged.

Carcinogens such as tobacco and alcohol, or a diet high in fat and low in fiber can increase the risk of colon cancer.

Carcinogens that can increase the risk of colorectal cancer over time include tobacco smoking, alcohol in excess, and some substances in the diet. Eating a diet that is high in fat and low in fiber has been shown to increase the risk of colon cancer in some medical studies. Other studies suggest that eating a lot of red meat or processed meat (such as hot dogs or bologna) may also increase colon cancer risk, either because of chemicals used to process the meats or because of chemicals that are formed by the way these meats are cooked. The chemicals may be carcinogenic. None of the studies about foods and colon cancer prove that diet causes cancer; they demonstrate only that some dietary choices may be a risk factor for colon cancer. Other lifestyle choices that may increase the risk of developing colon cancer are inactivity and lack of exercise and being significantly overweight. Whether these factors are tied to a poor diet is unclear to scientists. Whether colon cancer runs in families because they all eat a high fat, low fiber diet high in red meat is also unclear. Scientists also do not know whether there are other carcinogens that can increase risk for colon cancer.

The Risk Factor of Polyps

It is unknown to scientists why a lack of physical activity can increase the risk for colon cancer, but in a 2011 study scientist Kathleen Wolin and her research team discovered that regular exercise significantly reduced the risk of developing polyps in the colon. Wolin says, "We've long known that an active lifestyle can protect against bowel cancer, but this study is the first to look at all the available evidence and to show that a reduction in bowel polyps is the most likely explanation for this."[17] Wolin explains that exercise helps make the immune system stronger, helps prevent inflammation in the GI tract, and lowers the level of insulin in the blood. Insulin is a hormone that helps the body convert sugar to energy. When too much insulin is in the blood, the GI tract can become inflamed. Inflammation in the GI tract and a weak immune system that fails to attack damaged cells are known to increase the risk of developing colon polyps. Polyps, specifically adenomas, are the greatest risk factor for colon cancer.

Screening for Polyps and Preventing Cancer

Just as doctors are often uncertain about what causes colon cancer, it is also not clear why adenomas begin to grow in the colon. Researchers can identify risk factors such as lack of exercise, but they do not yet know the true cause of adenomas. They do not know why some adenomas become cancerous and some do not. However, since most colorectal cancer begins with these polyps, doctors refer to them as precancerous. They are not yet cancer, but they look abnormal and are likely to develop into cancer. This means that identifying and diagnosing polyps can be the way to drastically reduce the risk of colon cancer. Say the

Mayo Clinic doctors, "Removing polyps . . . before they become cancerous can prevent colon cancer."[18]

Polyps usually can be diagnosed with a medical screening test. A screening test is any medical test performed on a seemingly healthy individual in order to identify the presence of a disease or abnormality. It is meant to detect problems even though there are no signs or symptoms of disease and thereby to catch any disease process early and before it can do harm. Screening tests for colorectal cancer can catch polyps and abnormal cells before they become cancerous. The American Cancer Society says, "Early detection for colorectal cancer is the cornerstone of preventing this disease, since identifying and removing adenomatous polyps [adenomas] can decrease colorectal cancer by 60 to 90 percent."[19] The American Cancer Society and other medical organizations recommend that everyone over the age of fifty should be screened for polyps and colorectal cancer regularly. In addition, people with colon cancer in their families or who have other risk factors for colorectal cancer should be screened at earlier ages.

The Colonoscopy

Several screening methods for detecting polyps are available, but the most accurate medical test is called a colonoscopy. This medical test is usually performed by a gastroenterologist—a doctor who specializes in diseases of the gastrointestinal tract. The gastroenterologist uses a tool called a colonoscope to view the colon and rectum. It is a long, flexible tube with a tiny camera and light attached to the end. The camera is connected to a television monitor so that the doctor can view and inspect the entire lining of the colon and rectum. A patient undergoing colonoscopy usually has to undergo what is called a bowel prep. This means preparing on the day before the test with laxatives and a clear liquid diet in order to cleanse the bowel of stool so that the doctor can see the intestinal lining clearly. Right before the test, the patient is given a mild sedative through a needle inserted into a vein (an IV) so as to prevent any discomfort during the procedure. If

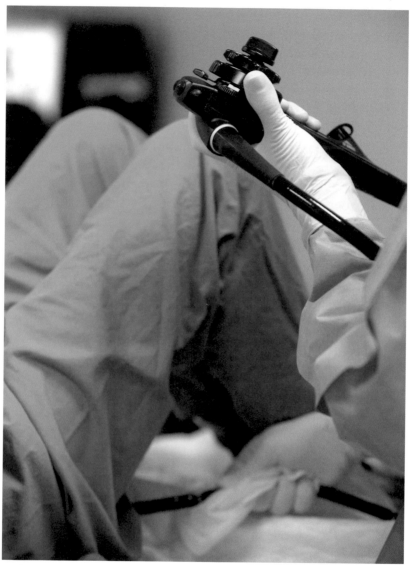

A doctor performs a colonoscopy screening test for colorectal cancer polyps and abnormal cells in the gastrointestinal tract.

the colonoscopy reveals any polyps, the doctor can remove a small sample for testing by passing small forceps through the tube of the colonoscope. This tissue sample can be examined in the laboratory, under a microscope, for the presence of abnormal cells. However, many times the doctor simply removes the polyp during the colonoscopy. The doctor passes a small wire loop through the colonoscope and uses it to snare and cut the polyp from the colon lining. A tiny electric current is also passed through the wire to seal off the small wound. Then the whole polyp can be examined in the laboratory for cancerous or precancerous cells.

Once a precancerous polyp is gone from the colon, it cannot develop into any kind of cancer. No matter how often polyps grow in an individual's colon, if they are regularly identified and removed early enough, progression to cancer cannot occur. Cindy, for example, is a fifty-eight-year-old woman whose mother died of colon cancer. Because of her family history, Cindy's doctor recommended that she undergo a colonoscopy regularly. Twice since she turned fifty, Cindy has had a colonoscopy. She reports, "I had polyps both times and they were removed during the colonoscopy. I didn't have any symptoms at all . . . this proves how valuable screening for colorectal cancer is. While I don't know for certain that the polyps would have turned into cancer, I'm glad I won't have the chance to find out!"[20]

Other Screening Tests

Cindy thinks that the unpleasantness of preparing for and undergoing a colonoscopy is well worth it, and a colonoscopy is the most sensitive kind of screening test for polyps. Although it may miss some very small polyps, it is more than 90 percent accurate at diagnosing adenomas. Nevertheless, since it is an invasive procedure that requires sedation, other, less-invasive and quicker diagnostic tests are sometimes used to screen for polyps. Since about half of all polyps are found in the last 2 feet (61 cm) of the colon, some doctors will screen for them using a test called flexible sigmoidoscopy. With a slender, shorter, lighted tube, the doctor looks at the rectum and last portion of the colon for signs of polyps. The test does not require sedation and is less invasive than a colonoscopy, but it can be a little uncomfortable and does still require a bowel prep. If any polyps are found, the doctor must follow up with

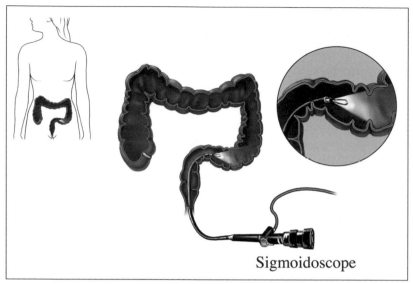

Sigmoidoscope

In a sigmoidoscopy test, a doctor uses a slender lighted tube to look into the patient's rectum and last portion of the colon for signs of polyps.

a colonoscopy to examine the entire colon and to remove the polyps.

One of the newer screening tests for polyps is a method of virtually examining the colon that is not invasive at all. This test, called computerized tomographic colonography (CTC), is a sensitive X-ray technique that uses computer imaging so that the doctor can see all areas of the colon. It is a quick and comfortable test, but doctors and researchers are unsure as yet that it is as accurate as a colonoscopy. It may miss some polyps, and that may mean missing the chance to prevent cancer from developing. If the CTC scan does reveal any polyps, a colonoscopy is still necessary so that the doctor can remove them and take samples for laboratory examination.

When Screening Finds Cancer

Diagnosing and removing polyps early can prevent colon cancer, but sometimes, by the time a screening test is done, the cells in the polyps have already become cancerous, meaning that the individual has already developed colon cancer. That is why doctors always send tissue samples of a polyp to a laboratory for further examination. Usually, this laboratory testing reveals perfectly normal cells, but sometimes malignant cancer cells may be detected. Also, if the doctor sees what appears to be abnormal tissue in the lining of the colon during the colonoscopy, he or she may take samples and send them for laboratory testing. These samples may indicate the presence of cancer cells, too. Diagnosis of colorectal cancer commonly begins with a colonoscopy, tissue samples, and laboratory testing. Most often, a specialist called a pathologist microscopically examines the tissue samples, visually identifies the presence of cancer cells, and attempts to determine the type and extent of the cancer. For example, the pathologist may need to determine that the cancer cells in colon tissue are colon cancer cells rather than cancer cells that arose in another organ and traveled to the colon.

Once colorectal cancer cells have been identified, the next step in the diagnosis of colorectal cancer is to determine its

Doctors and nurses view a monitor while performing a colonoscopy procedure on a patient. Pathologists will analyze samples of tissues collected to identify cancerous cells.

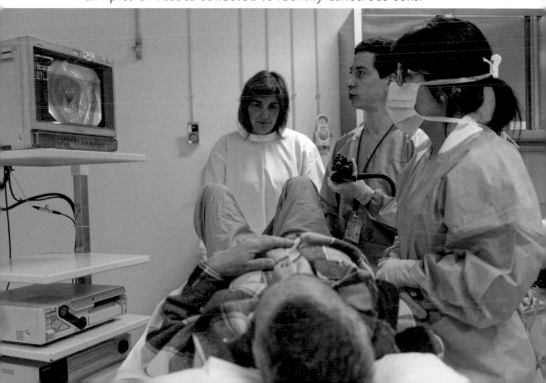

stage and grade. Usually this means that the doctor does a physical examination and orders further medical tests. With a digital rectal exam, the doctor examines the anal opening and also examines the groin area to look for any sign of enlarged lymph nodes. Enlarged lymph nodes may indicate that the cancer has spread. He or she then feels the abdominal area to determine whether any masses, growths, or enlarged organs are evidcnt. These markers may also indicate that the cancer has spread. Blood tests can be used along with a physical examination to identify a colorectal cancer tumor marker called carcinoembryonic antigen (CEA). It is a protein that appears in the blood and can signify that there is cancer somewhere in the body. Not everyone with colon cancer has this tumor

Ethnic Groups and Colon Cancer

According to the Centers for Disease Control and Prevention (CDC), different ethnic groups in the United States have different risks of developing and dying from colon cancer. In 2007 (the latest date for which the CDC has statistics), the ethnic group with the highest incidence of colorectal cancer was African Americans. The second highest rate was in Caucasians. Next highest were Hispanics, then Native Americans, and finally Asians and Pacific Islanders. The rates of death from colorectal cancer followed the same pattern.

Scientists are uncertain about why the rates of colorectal cancer vary among ethnic groups, but in 2011 one study suggested that the differences might be due in part to screening rates. The researchers looked at people on Medicare between seventy and eighty-nine years old and found that the Caucasians were more likely to get screening tests for polyps than were African Americans or Hispanics. The researchers concluded that marker, but when the cancer is advanced or has spread, it may be detected.

Several different kinds of imaging tests are available, and they are the most important methods used to diagnose the stage of cancer. The American Cancer Society explains, "These tests are used to make images or pictures of the cancer and look for evidence of spread of the tumor."[21] Imaging tests include X-rays of the chest to check for spots on the lungs where the cancer may have spread and computed tomography (CT or CAT scan) of the abdomen and chest to check for spread of the cancer to the lungs or liver. A magnetic resonance imaging (MRI) test uses radio waves and a magnet to get pictures of the body, especially of the brain and spine, to determine if

more medical effort is needed to persuade older people of all ethnic groups who are on Medicare to be screened and perhaps prevent colorectal cancer.

Incidence Rates by Race

Race/Ethnicity	Male	Female
All Races	55.0 per 100,000 men	41.0 per 100,000 women
White	54.4 per 100,000 men	40.2 per 100,000 women
Black	67.7 per 100,000 men	51.2 per 100,000 women
Asian/Pacific Islander	45.4 per 100,000 men	34.6 per 100,000 women
American Indian/Alaska Native*	42.7 per 100,000 men	40.0 per 100,000 women
Hispanic**	46.0 per 100,000 men	32.3 per 100,000 women

*Incidence data for Hispanics is based on NHIA (NAACCR Hispanic Identification Algorithm) and excludes cases from Alaska Native Registry. Hispanic death rates exclude deaths from the District of Columbia and North Dakota.
**Incidence and mortality data for American Indians/Alaska Natives is based on the CHSDA (Contract Health Service Delivery Area) counties.

Taken from: http://seer.cancer.gov.

the tissues look normal. Positron emission tomography (PET) is a test in which radioactive sugar is injected into a vein and then a scanner measures how quickly the cells in the body absorb the sugar. This imaging test works because cancer cells use more energy than normal cells and absorb the sugar more quickly. With PET scans, doctors can identify cancer cells that do not show up in CT scans or MRIs.

All of the imaging tests are valuable for diagnosing colon cancer that has metastasized or spread to other areas of the body (stage IV), but determining the earlier stages of cancer, especially whether it has spread to lymph nodes (stage III), requires lymph node sampling. In a minor surgical procedure called a biopsy, the doctor removes either whole lymph nodes or samples from at least twelve lymph nodes in the general area of the cancer tumor. These samples or nodes are sent to the pathologist who checks each one for evidence of cancer cells. The results of the lymph node sampling tell the doctors whether further testing of lymph nodes is necessary and whether surgery is likely to be necessary to treat the cancer. Often, until surgical treatment is performed after a diagnosis of colon cancer, doctors are unsure of the exact cancer stage. So surgery can be a part of both diagnosis and treatment. Making the best and most appropriate treatment decisions—based on the cancer's stage—is the goal of all diagnostic tests for colorectal cancer.

CHAPTER THREE

Treatment of Colon Cancer

Treatment of colorectal cancer depends primarily on the stage of the disease and includes four main treatment methods. They are surgery, chemotherapy, radiation therapy, and targeted therapy (using drugs and other substances to specifically attack cancer cells). The National Cancer Institute reports, "Cancer of the colon is a highly treatable and often curable disease when localized to the bowel."[22] Even when the cancer has metastasized, it can often be effectively treated with a combination of treatment methods.

Surgical Treatment

Except for some stage IV colon cancers, surgery is almost always the first treatment choice. With stage 0 cancer, when the cells have not spread beyond the inner lining of the colon, simple surgery to remove the polyp may be all that is necessary to cure the cancer. In this case, the doctor performs a polypectomy; it is the same procedure as a colonoscopy, in which the whole polyp is cut from the lining of the colon. Sometimes, however, the polyp is so large that it cannot be removed—or excised—so easily, and more invasive surgery is needed. Then, in a procedure called a colectomy, a surgeon may have to remove the piece of the colon in which the polyp is growing. This means removing the polyp and a margin of

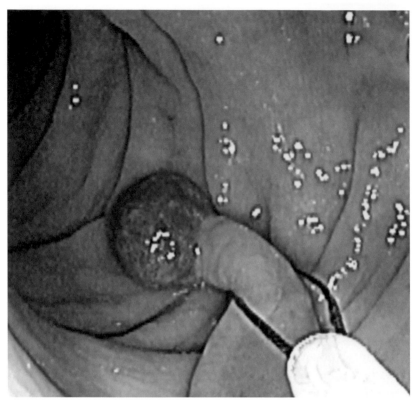

Doctors perform anal polyp removal surgery. Except for some stage IV colon cancers, surgery is almost always the first choice for treatment.

healthy tissue surrounding the polyp, just to be completely sure that no abnormal cells are left behind. Afterward, the surgeon sews the two healthy ends of the colon back together. The surgery to remove the portion of colon is called a resection, and the rejoining is called anastomosis.

About 96 percent of people with stage 0 colorectal cancer are cured by surgical treatment. A cure of cancer is defined by medical professionals as disease-free survival for five years after treatment is completed. This means there is no recurrence of any cancer and no need for further treatment. The five-year disease-free survival rate is not a guarantee of a cure because no one knows for sure that a cancer will not return many years later. However, with stage 0 colorectal cancer, the chances are excellent that the individual will be cured by the surgical treatment. Regular follow-up screening for polyps may be all that is required for a person who has had stage 0 colon cancer. Cynthia, for example, had a cancerous polyp in her colon in 1987, when she was thirty-five years old. She had the HNPCC gene mutation in her family and so had a colonoscopy. She says it saved her life. She remembers, "We had found the polyp so early that the cancer was across the top of the polyp. This meant that a surgeon could remove the threat by doing a . . . colectomy."[23] On the website Colon Cancer Alliance, Cynthia reports that she continues to remain cancer free today.

When colon cancer is in stage I, resection and anastomosis are the standard treatment, and, usually, no other treatment is needed because the cancer has not spread outside the outer wall of the colon. Many cases of stage II colon cancer also can be treated with surgical resection and anastomosis. When cancer has spread to nearby lymph nodes, in stage III, resection and anastomosis are used to destroy all the cancer cells within the colon, but the surgeon must also surgically remove the affected lymph nodes. With stage IV cancer, resection and anastomosis of the colon cannot remove all the cancer because it has spread to other organs. If possible, surgery is performed to remove any tumor in these other organs, such as liver, lungs, or ovaries. Even if the cancer cannot be removed from other organs, resection and anastomosis in the colon can remove any obstructions or blockages caused by a large tumor. The resection for all these stages of cancer includes removing a large portion of healthy colon on either side of the tumor—usually 12 inches (30.1cm) or more—to be certain that no cancer cells are left behind.

Surgery and Ostomies

Sometimes, when a large portion of the colon has been surgically removed, the rest of the healthy colon needs time to heal. In that case, the surgeon may perform a temporary colostomy or ileostomy to prevent waste or stool from moving through the colon, allowing the colon to rest and recover. In

The J-Pouch

J-pouch surgery is a new advancement in treatment that can help some people avoid the need for a permanent ostomy. Sixty-one-year-old Sharon Tschider, for example, had J-pouch surgery after her rectal cancer was diagnosed. Her surgeon, Bruce Wolff of the Mayo Clinic, decided that she had to have a resection and anastomosis for the large tumor. Then, he fashioned a pouch for her—inside her body rather than outside as with an ostomy—so that she would be able to go to the bathroom relatively normally. He explains, "To do this, I turned the colon around on itself and created a pouch shaped like a 'J' that would eventually prevent the need for a colostomy bag." Tschider had to have a temporary ileostomy to use until the J-pouch healed. Then, Wolff reversed the ileostomy and reconnected her colon to the pouch. Her waste went through her remaining colon to be stored in the pouch and then to be eliminated through her anus in the usual way. Tschider had to get used to the pouch, but three years later, she eliminates her wastes comfortably and is active, healthy, and cancer-free.

Quoted in American Society of Colon & Rectal Surgeons. "Colorectal Cancer Patient Sharon Tschider." Patient Success Stories. www.fascrs.org/patients/patient _success_stories/colorectal_cancer_patient_sharon_tschider.

a colostomy, one end of the cut colon is brought through an opening made in the wall of the abdomen. In an ileostomy, the entire colon is bypassed, and the end of the ileum (the lowest part of the small intestine) is brought to the abdominal opening. In either type of ostomy, the opening is called a stoma. A bag attached to the stoma collects body wastes. Instead of going to the bathroom in the typical way, a person with an ostomy empties the bag. After about two or three months (but sometimes after as long as a year), the whole

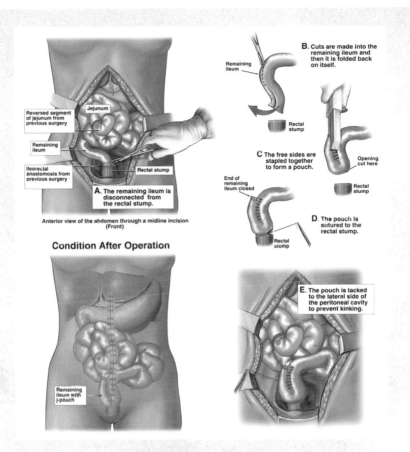

An illustration shows a surgical illeorectal anastomosis construction of a J-Pouch. It is a new advancement that can help some people avoid a permanent ostomy.

colon has healed, and the surgeon reverses the ostomy, putting the two ends of the colon or the colon and intestine back together. Most commonly, a temporary colostomy is needed for treating cancer in the ascending or transverse colon. An ileostomy may be used when the cancer has to be cut out at the juncture where the colon and small intestine meet.

At other times, people with colon cancer may need a permanent ostomy. This is sometimes needed when the cancer is in the descending or sigmoid colon or in the rectum. The cancer may have invaded these areas so significantly that they must be completely removed in order to save the person's life. Darrick Price, for instance, was diagnosed with a rare colon cancer at the end of his colon when he was just sixteen years old. He explains, "Because the tumor destroyed the muscle near my rectum I had to have a colostomy, where doctors remove some of your colon and create an opening in your abdomen, from which you drain your stool."[24] Eighteen years after his cancer diagnosis, in 2005, Price reported that the surgery to remove the affected segments of his colon and rectum completely cured his colon cancer. He continues to see his doctor for regular checkups, but he is in perfect health. For people with genetic mutations that cause polyps and cancer in the colon, removal of the colon and living with an ileostomy also greatly reduces the risk of colon cancer returning in the future.

Chemotherapy Treatment

Surgery is an important treatment method for colon cancer, but for any cancer that may have spread—whether through the colon, to lymph nodes, or to other organs—further treatment is necessary to ensure, as far as possible, that no cancer cells remain in the body. Otherwise, the cancer will recur. Chemotherapy is the standard treatment method for any colon cancer in stages III or IV and often for stage II as well. Chemotherapy is the use of drugs to destroy cancer cells. It can kill cancer cells that cannot be removed surgically or that surgery has missed. The American Cancer Society explains the need for chemotherapy this way: "Even when it appears that all cancer has been removed, microscopic cancer cells may still remain, either in the place that the tumor was removed or as micrometastases to other parts of the body."[25] Chemotherapy used after surgery to kill any cancerous cells that may have been missed is called adjuvant chemotherapy treatment. When it is used because surgery is not an option because the cancer has spread and cannot be eliminated surgically, it is called primary chemotherapy. The chemotherapy drugs are given through a needle inserted into a vein (an IV) or in pill form. In either case, the medicine travels through the bloodstream, essentially poisoning cancer cells throughout the body.

How much chemotherapy is needed and for how long depends on the stage and grade of the cancer. A typical course of chemotherapy for colon cancer is six months. The medicine is administered regularly, perhaps daily or weekly, with breaks in between to give the body a chance to rest and recover. This is necessary because chemotherapy is not just poisonous to cancer cells but also to normal body cells. Chemotherapy drugs kill cancer cells by attacking cells that rapidly divide (which all cancer cells do); however normal cells that frequently and regularly divide, such as blood cells, cells in the membrane of the mouth and GI tract, and hair cells, are also attacked.

Chemotherapy drugs are given through a needle inserted into a vein or in pill form. Medicine travels through the bloodstream to poison cancer cells throughout the body.

The most common chemotherapy drug used to treat colon cancer is called 5-FU (5-fluorouracil). It is administered through an IV and is usually combined with a vitamin preparation called leucovorin, which helps 5-FU work better. 5-FU works by preventing cells from making DNA and RNA in order to divide and multiply. This means that cancer cells cannot spread, but it also means that chemotherapy can cause unpleasant side effects as it damages normal cells. People receiving 5-FU may experience nausea, weakness, loss of hair, a loss of red blood cells, diarrhea, mouth sores, and rashes. Brian, for example, is a fifty-three-year-old man in Australia who was diagnosed with stage IV colon cancer in May 2011. Brian's cancer had spread to his lungs and his liver. The spots in both organs were operable, and a bowel resection could be performed for the colon tumor itself. Chemotherapy was necessary, however, because there was no way to know where else cancer cells may have spread. Brian says, "The chemotherapy has certainly been an experience. So far I have experienced nausea and vomiting during the five weeks of 5FU. It caused both my lips to be totally ulcerated, along with mouth ulcers and irregular bowel motions. The worst side effects were . . . soon controlled with anti-nausea medications."[26]

Radiation Therapy

Brian also required treatment with radiation therapy. "Radiation therapy," explains the Mayo Clinic "uses powerful energy sources, such as X-rays, to kill any cancer cells that might remain after surgery, to shrink large tumors before an operation so that they can be removed more easily, or to relieve symptoms of colon cancer and rectal cancer."[27] The radiation is commonly delivered outside the body with an X-ray machine aimed directly at the area of the tumor. The goal is to kill cancer cells, but normal cells are killed by radiation, too. By targeting the cancer cells, doctors strive to kill as few normal cells as possible, but inevitably, some normal cells are damaged, and this causes side effects. The most typical side effects of radiation are fatigue, diarrhea, nausea, and skin irritation

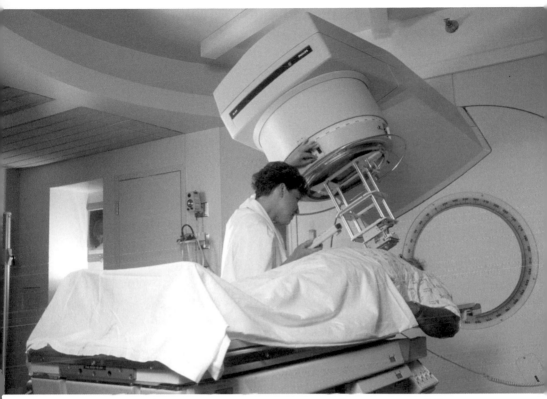

Radiation therapy uses energy sources such as X-rays to kill cancer cells that may remain after surgery, to relieve symptoms of colon and rectal cancer, or to shrink large tumors before surgery.

at the treatment site. Brian experienced only the fatigue from his radiation therapy. In Brian's case, radiation treatment was used to shrink the tumor in his colon before surgery because a smaller tumor is easier to remove than a larger one. He had radiation therapy five days a week for five weeks. He is still undergoing treatment for his cancer and will have more treatment in the future, but he feels that all the side effects are tolerable because he plans to beat the cancer.

Gillian, a sixty-two-year-old Australian woman had radiation therapy as part of her colon cancer treatment, also. When her colon cancer was diagnosed she was fifty-eight years old. Her doctors first treated her with chemotherapy and radiation therapy for five weeks. Once her large tumor had shrunk from this treatment, her surgeon performed a bowel resection. Then, she received another round of chemotherapy with 5-FU. Today, it appears that Gillian's treatment regimen has succeeded. She says, "I still have quarterly check-ups [every three months], which will go down to once every six months after my next visit, and so far I remain cancer-free."[28] If all goes well, after five years of regular checkups she will be considered cured of her cancer.

Targeted Therapy

Brian and Gillian each had the traditional treatment program for colon cancer—surgery, chemotherapy, and radiation—but today, the newest form of treatment for colon cancer includes targeted therapy. Unlike regular chemotherapy which can affect all body cells, targeted therapy is the use of drugs or other substances to target only cancer cells. This is possible because the gene mutations that allow a cell to become cancerous also cause changes in some protein molecules

Targeted therapy uses specifically tailored drugs and other substances to target cancer cells by attacking their specific protein molecules.

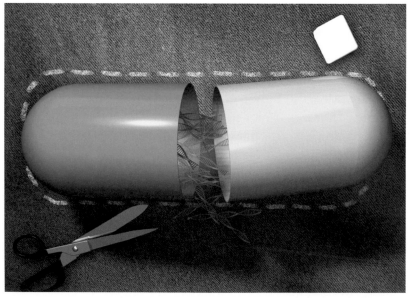

in the cells that are unique to cancer. Normal cells do not have these changed protein molecules. The goal of targeted therapy is to destroy cancer cells by attacking their specific protein molecules. For this reason, targeted therapy is also known as molecularly targeted therapy. In the laboratory, scientists develop what are known as small-molecule drugs and artificial antibodies that can enter into a cell and damage or destroy the protein molecule that determines the cell's activity. The website CancerConnect.com explains, "Some targeted therapies block growth signals from reaching cancer cells; others reduce the blood supply to cancer cells; and still others stimulate the immune system to recognize and attack the cancer cell. Depending on the specific 'target,' targeted therapies may slow cancer cell growth or increase cancer cell death."[29]

Targeted therapy is so specific to different kinds of cancer cells, however, that many therapies that work with some kinds of cancer have no effect on other kinds. The targeted therapy that destroys breast cancer cells, for example, is useless for colon cancer cells. Researchers believe that this difference may be related to which mutated genes allow the cancer to develop in the first place. Today, three targeted therapy drugs are approved for use to treat colorectal cancer. They are bevacizumab, cetuximab, and panitumumab. These drugs target the growth factors—the proteins that direct cells to divide and multiply—in cancer cells. Bevacizumab interferes with the ability of the tumor to grow new blood vessels. Cetuximab and panitumumab interfere with the cancer cell's ability to receive signals to grow and divide. All three drugs are used primarily for people with stage IV cancer who have not gotten better with chemotherapy. Sometimes, the targeted therapy may also be combined with standard chemotherapy to treat stage IV cancer in order to give the person the best chance for a successful treatment outcome.

Targeted therapy treatments are so new that researchers are still learning about how and when to use them. According to the Mayo Clinic, "Some people are helped by targeted drugs, while others are not."[30] Sometimes, cancer cells can develop a resistance to the drugs. At other times, the cell mutations that caused the cancer to develop are unknown and so are not appropriately targeted by the drug. Medical researchers continue to try to learn which kinds of colon tumors or metastases respond best to which targeted therapy. Colon cancer treatment is a rapidly evolving area of medicine, and many new treatments and targeted therapies are being developed, tested, and evaluated on an ongoing basis. This means that even a person with an aggressive, stage IV cancer for whom surgery, radiation, chemotherapy, and approved targeted therapy have not worked may have other treatment options available.

Experimental Treatment and Clinical Trials

Often, people choose to join a clinical trial to get access to the latest treatment if other treatment options have not produced results. The American Cancer Society explains, "Clinical trials are research studies in people. . . . Most clinical trials in the field of cancer deal with new drugs or new combinations of drugs to treat cancer."[31] These drugs are being considered for approval for medical use, and the trials help researchers determine any possible side effects or other problems with the treatment, as well as how effective the drugs are. By participating in a clinical trial, a person can get treatment that is unavailable anywhere else. The treatment may not only help the person but may also lead to improved treatment for other people in the future. Because of clinical trials, for example, five new chemotherapy drugs other than 5-FU have been approved for use with colon cancer patients in the United States since 1990. People who participated in clinical trials also helped researchers identify the targeted therapies for colon cancer that are in use today.

John Peterson participated in a clinical trial in 2007 to test a new kind of treatment for metastatic colon cancer with what are called radioactive microspheres. Peterson was first treated for colon cancer in 2001, when he had a cancerous

A colored scanning electron micrograph shows drug delivery microspheres. These tiny plastic beads filled with radioactive substances are injected into the body via catheter to the cancerous area.

polyp removed. For six years he was cancer free, but the cancer recurred in 2007. This time, it had metastasized. Peterson had three cancerous lymph nodes and two cancerous spots in his liver. The tumors that were deep inside his liver could not be removed surgically. Peterson began chemotherapy, but his prognosis (predicted outcome) was still poor. Peterson's doctors did not expect the chemotherapy to save his life. Peterson says, "I decided to participate in the clinical trial because it offered me hope. To me, this trial was offering another chance at life when so many people were preparing me for death."[32]

In the trial, the doctors inserted a tube called a catheter into an artery in Peterson's leg and then threaded it into the artery in his liver that supplied the tumors with blood. They injected microspheres—tiny plastic beads filled with a radioactive substance—through the catheter and into Peterson's liver close to the tumors. The microspheres worked. Three weeks after the experimental treatment, a PET scan showed no sign of cancer cells in Peterson's liver. Peterson continued to receive chemotherapy and was cancer free for a year, but then his cancer recurred in his pelvic cavity, in his liver, and as one tumor in his lung. In 2009, after more chemotherapy, Peterson seemed to be beating his recurrent cancer once again. X-rays showed that the new tumors had disappeared with standard chemotherapy treatment.

An Ongoing Effort

Peterson's experience demonstrates how difficult it can be to treat metastasized cancer successfully. If even one cancer cell has escaped the treatment, that cell may travel anywhere and grow into a tumor. Nevertheless, Peterson was glad that he had participated in the clinical trial. He says, "I might not have been alive to continue to fight against cancer if I had not participated in the clinical trial."[33]

Today, the microsphere treatment that Peterson received is called Selective Internal Radiation Therapy (SIRT). SIRT is used regularly for people with inoperable metastasized colon

Alternative Treatments

Conventional or standard cancer treatments, such as radiation, chemotherapy, and surgery, are therapies that have been medically studied and proven to be effective against cancer. Alternative treatments are those that have shown little or no evidence of effectiveness or safety. Examples include so-called cancer cures such as electromagnetic therapy, which uses magnets or electromagnetic waves to correct a supposed electromagnetic field imbalance in the body, and metabolic therapies, which are based on special diets, vitamin and mineral supplements, and procedures for cleansing or detoxifying the body. The American Cancer Society warns that replacing conventional treatment with alternative treatment can be dangerous. Many alternative treatments exist, but they can be costly and give people false hope, when, in actuality, they have not been shown to prevent cancer, cure cancer, or even slow a cancer's growth. The American Cancer Society recommends that anyone considering an alternative treatment instead of a standard treatment check with a trusted medical expert such as a doctor, hospital, or government resource.

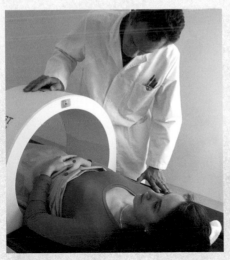

A doctor uses a pulsed electromagnetic field therapy to treat a patient with cancer. Because it is an alternative treatment method, its effectiveness remains unproven.

cancer, and further clinical trials are ongoing to determine the strongest but safest dose for SIRT treatment and to see how well it compares with other kinds of cancer treatments. People who participate in these trials and in other treatment trials know that the treatments may not save their lives, but clinical trials do give them hope. Coping with colon cancer can be hard because death is always a possibility, but the cancer therapies available today make living with colon cancer much more hopeful than it has ever been before.

CHAPTER FOUR

Living with Colon Cancer

Living with colon cancer can be frightening and difficult. Receiving the diagnosis of cancer scares almost everyone. Going through colon cancer treatment can be unpleasant, uncomfortable, and sometimes life-changing. The outcome of treatment is uncertain, and even when treatment is over, people's lives can seem permanently changed. Nevertheless, most people face colon cancer and its effects with courage, and many are able to treat it successfully.

The Shock of Diagnosis

When Jessie Gruman was fifty years old, in 2003, she was diagnosed with colon cancer. She had already been through three terrifying medical experiences. At age twenty, she was diagnosed with Hodgkin's disease, a cancer of the lymph nodes. At age thirty, she was diagnosed with cervical cancer, and at age forty, she developed a heart infection that almost killed her. Despite her experience with surviving and adjusting to all these medical crises, she says that hearing the diagnosis of colon cancer was extremely hard. Gruman's colon cancer was successfully treated with surgical resection and anastomosis, but she clearly remembers how devastating it was at first to try to face a life-threatening diagnosis. She explains, "What strikes you is the magnitude of the shock. . . . You don't know if you're

During the first two days after a colon cancer diagnosis, a patient must cope with the initial shock and gear up for what will come next.

going to live or die. You don't know what kind of pain you're going to face. . . . You don't know anything. Everything that was certain 10 minutes ago is not certain now."[34]

Gruman believes that the first two days after the diagnosis are the hardest to get through because of coping with the initial shock and stress and having to decide what to do next. She is a social psychologist who understands the feelings that people need to overcome in order to live with a frightening disease. She says that people can have different reactions, but everyone has to find a way to face and come to terms with their illness. She says, "Some people rage against the unfairness while others wither from sadness. Some people lose their faith and others find it. Some are torn between their fear of pain and their fear of death. Families are wracked by the threat of loss. It is a time when nothing is certain, and the future looks dark."[35]

Coping with the Diagnosis

In 2007 Gruman wrote a book about her own experience and the experiences of others who have dealt with terrifying diagnoses. She named the book *AfterShock* and writes not only about the initial emotions of shock and fear but also about how to handle the first forty-eight hours after the cancer is diagnosed. She says, for example, that people need to take the first two days to absorb the bad news of the diagnosis and not go to work or school, be sure to eat and sleep, and give themselves permission to cry or grieve if they need to. Her most important piece of advice is, "Remember: You will not always feel like this."[36]

The American Cancer Society agrees with Gruman that shock and disbelief are the first common reactions when people are diagnosed with cancer, but after these feelings wear off, people often go through a series of emotional steps as they go through treatment and come to grips with fighting a life-threatening disease. Some of these emotions are anger, grief, fear, feeling isolated and alone, and depression. About 25 percent of people diagnosed with cancer suffer depression, according to the American Cancer Society. Other people may become so anxious that they have panic attacks or cannot function normally. Those with anxiety or depression need to seek medical or psychological help for these issues as well as for the cancer. Whatever the emotions, however, most people eventually learn to face the reality of their colon cancer and fight to get well. The American Cancer Society says, "Sometimes, there's no better way to cope with a problem than to do something about it. You may not be able to make your cancer disappear, but there are many things you can do to take control of your situation and cope with your disease."[37]

On a forum for people who have survived stage IV colon cancer, one man describes how he coped and took control of his disease at the age of forty-five, in 1995. He turned to family and friends for support and talked to a psychologist to help himself become optimistic about treatment and to believe that he could heal. He says, "I was in a fog for a while." Then he started to fight. He remembers, "I tried to stay focused on making the cancer go away. In order to do this, I had to get my anger and worry behind me and get to work."[38] With a treatment combination of surgery and chemotherapy that lasted more than a year, this man did win his fight against colon cancer. He is a cancer survivor and feels very grateful to be alive despite the emotional and physical difficulties that he faced throughout the treatment.

When diagnosed with any kind of cancer, people often experience similar emotional reactions while they go through treatment and come to grips with a life-threatening disease. Anger, grief, fear, isolation, and loneliness are just some of these emotions.

A Coping Strategy That Works

Living with colon cancer treatments can be a struggle. Treatments can cause side effects, disrupt people's normal lives, and sometimes require permanent body changes, such as ostomies. Even when the treatment is relatively straightforward and quick, people may struggle with the fear that the cancer will recur. In 2003, for example, then forty-nine-year-old fashion designer Carmen Marc Valvo had a colonoscopy that revealed a "lemon-sized" cancerous tumor. Valvo had surgery to remove the tumor, but no one could be sure for a year whether the cancer would recur and require radiation or chemotherapy treatments. As he waited and went through medical checkups to be certain he was cured, Valvo was worried and anxious about his future. He turned to two activities, he says, to help himself stay calm and positive. "One was my fashion design, and the second was my garden," he remembers. "That summer, I was in the garden non-stop. I wanted to see things grow and blossom, and that helped me, physically, overcome my anxiety, my fear." Valvo's colon cancer was gone, and in 2008 he revealed to the world that he was a colon cancer survivor. Today, he tries to help others to beat colon cancer, too. He says, "It's a cancer that is so curable if detected early. It's something not to be afraid of. Knowledge is definitely power."[39]

Treatment's Long, Hard Road

When colon cancer is not caught early, coping with treatment is much more complicated than it was for Valvo. Phil Gagler, for instance, was diagnosed with stage IV colon cancer, and the first doctor who diagnosed him did not think Gagler could survive. Gagler was unwilling to accept that prognosis and was committed to "showing cancer who's the boss." With a new team of doctors, he began a long, courageous battle. First he had six months of chemotherapy to shrink the tumors in his colon, gall bladder, and liver. During this time, he began kayaking to build up his strength for his upcoming surgery. He kayaked every day before going to work for eighty-one days in a row. Then he had surgery to remove the section of his colon where the tumor was. At the same time, the surgeon removed his gall bladder and 60 percent of his liver. After the surgery, chemotherapy began again. Doctors surgically implanted a small pump through which the chemotherapy drugs could be directly delivered to his liver. Then, doctors found that the cancer cells had spread to Gagler's lungs. Over the next three years, Gagler had three lung surgeries to remove the tumors and more chemotherapy. Altogether, Gagler had chemotherapy 260 times. Still, he remains determined and optimistic, and he endures all the treatments with patience. He says, "I had to accept that things happen when they happen. When I'm done, I'm done. When I'm not, I'm not. . . . Cancer gives you a lot of new normal. I was normal before this happened. Then chemo was a new normal to get used to. Surgery—another new normal to get used to."[40] As of 2012 Gagler is still receiving regular chemotherapy treatments for his metastases, but he is living a normal, active life. At fifty-four years old, he has been fighting cancer for seven years, and he is winning.

Side Effects

Though Gagler found the fatigue and nausea that usually accompany chemotherapy treatment tolerable, many patients struggle with the side effects of treatment. Claudia, who was diagnosed with colorectal cancer in 2004, had serious trouble with the side effects from both radiation and chemotherapy. She had six months of chemotherapy that left her with painful canker sores in her mouth, and she was so nauseated that she vomited whenever she tried to eat. She says she lost more than 100 pounds (45.36kg) during her treatment. After five months of chemotherapy, she also began radiation therapy, and her nausea got worse. She says she got so sick that she could eat almost nothing. The result was that she got so weak that she could not walk and had to use a wheelchair.

Claudia continued with her treatments, despite her suffering, until she was able to have surgery to remove her tumor. Then, she seemed to get better, even though her doctors were worried that they had not removed all the cancer cells. Her

Walking the Sadness Away

Facing a colon cancer diagnosis and coping with treatment side effects often can be made easier with exercise. Sally, a fifty-year-old woman with stage II colon cancer, had to have a months-long course of chemotherapy. The treatment was making her weak and exhausted, and she became sad and depressed. Regular exercise made all the difference in Sally's will to live. She says, "I felt like life was closing in on me. I didn't want to go out and see my friends or do anything. Then my neighbor friend took me for a walk. Wow! There's no question that helped my mood. It was like I came out of my shell and saw the blue sky and brilliant green grass for the first time ever. The bird sounds were lovely. I feel much better about everything and I'm sleeping better too." The American Cancer Society recommends appropriate exercise, with a doctor's approval, as a good way for people to relieve stress and anxiety, ease depression, increase their energy, and even improve their appetites while they are undergoing cancer treatment.

Quoted in Anna L. Schwartz. *Cancer Fitness.* New York: Fireside, Simon & Schuster, 2004, p. 24.

Facing cancer diagnosis and coping with treatment side effects can often be made easier by exercising. It can relieve stress and anxiety, ease depression, increase the level of energy, and improve the appetite.

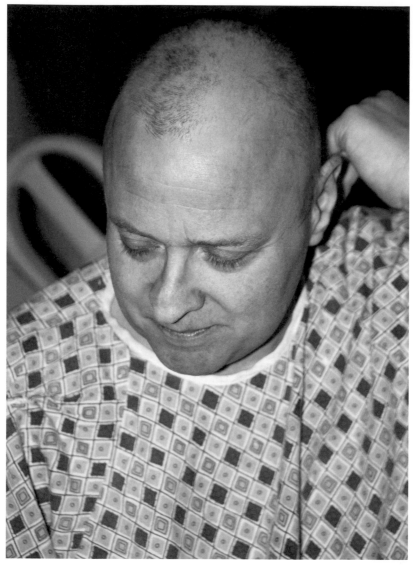

Side effects of cancer therapy include hair loss, nausea, appetite loss, and a general lack of strength.

other treatments had to continue. Then, in 2006 she began experiencing severe abdominal pain. Further surgery revealed that a rare complication had occurred. Claudia's intestines had been burned and damaged by her radiation therapy. She underwent another resection to remove the damaged part of her intestine. Claudia was finally cancer free, although doctors did not know yet if any cancer would recur. She had to continue to receive chemotherapy every six weeks, just to be safe. Despite what happened, however, Claudia believes that her treatments were worth enduring. She says, "I live with many side effects from all the treatment I have undergone, but the greatest gift I've received from this whole experience is that 'I'm Alive!'"[41]

Leaning on Others and Gaining Knowledge

Claudia endured her cancer treatment with courage and determination. When the ordeal was over, she joined the patient advocacy organization Colon Cancer Alliance to help others deal with colorectal cancer. She volunteers with the organization's online buddy program so that she can offer understanding, support, and encouragement to people in similar situations. Finding social and psychological support is a critical need for most people with colon cancer, whether newly diagnosed, under treatment, or successfully in remission (seemingly cancer free and with no more symptoms).

Many people turn to family and friends, and many also seek out others who have experienced living with cancer. At the American Cancer Society's Cancer Survivors Network, people with cancer and their families can anonymously share their experiences and find support from people who have had the same experiences and understand their feelings. Robert Hendrickson, for example, is a survivor of stage II colon cancer and a longtime member of the Cancer Survivors Network. He and the friends he found online there formed their own discussion group called the "Semi-Colons." Hendrickson had no friends or family nearby to help him through his cancer, so the Semi-Colons became his support group. Even after he completed treatment and showed no signs of cancer, he stayed with the online group to help others and stay connected. He says, "They're my good friends. They're my family. And I want to be there for people who are just starting the battle. I drew inspiration myself from people who were farther along."[42]

In addition to emotional support, the American Cancer Society also helps people educate themselves about their cancers. It helps them find practical tips about how to get through treatment ordeals and give themselves the best chance to become cancer survivors. Kathy Croswell took advantage of this outreach when she was diagnosed with colon cancer in 2000. She had surgery to remove the tumor in her colon and three cancerous lymph nodes. As she recovered from the surgery in the hospital, she called the American Cancer Society's toll-free helpline. She remembers,

> I spoke with a representative there and she was very helpful—she sent a booklet with all the facts about colon cancer, including a dictionary of terms, a primer on treatment and questions to ask about nutrition, what to ask the oncologist [cancer specialist] and even how to handle nutrition. That book helped me to not be afraid. I realized that the more educated you are, the better prepared. And because of the book, I knew what to expect.[43]

Coping with Food

Getting proper nutrition, staying active, and coping with fatigue can be difficult for people undergoing treatment for colon cancer. The American Cancer Society says, "Nutrition is an important part of cancer treatment. Eating the right kinds of foods before, during, and after treatment can help you feel better and stay stronger."[44] Eating may be a problem for people with colon cancer because of loss of appetite, nausea from treatment, or just being too tired to fix meals. Helen Taylor, for example, was diagnosed with stage IV colon cancer and treated with intense chemotherapy to kill the cells that had spread. She was so weak and tired that fixing meals was a huge chore. Taylor was a member of a kickboxing class, and her fellow class members pitched in and brought her hot meals after every chemotherapy session so that she did not have to worry about cooking for herself.

When nausea is the main problem, it can usually be managed—at least in part—with medications. Still, says colon cancer

Guidance for Family and Friends

When a loved one has colon cancer, family members and friends want to provide help and support, but they may not know what to do. The American Cancer Society says that people can help in both practical and emotional ways. Friends and family can offer a shoulder to cry on. They can be available for visits, chatting, watching movies together, playing games, or taking drives or short walks for fun. They can mail notes or cards of love and support. Practical help can involve cooking and cleaning chores when the person with cancer is too weak to cope with daily life. It can be walking the dog, doing laundry, or running errands. Sometimes, the person may need help with bathing or dressing or being driven to doctor's appointments.

Friends and family, however, also need to take care of themselves. The American Cancer Society recommends that they be careful to get plenty of rest, eat well, and exercise regularly. If they are struggling with painful emotions, such as fear or sadness, they should not be embarrassed to ask for help themselves, such as psychological counseling or joining support groups. Colon cancer is a difficult experience for everyone involved.

Friends and family can provide help and support to cancer patients. They can be a shoulder to cry on, be available for visits, spend quality time, and take short drives or walks for fun.

survivor Becky Kritz of her own struggles with nausea, "Life was far from normal. I had to take extra iron pills and have B-12 shots. I was on three types of antinausea medication."[45] Even with her antinausea medications, Kritz lost 55 pounds (24.9kg) during her treatment. She developed vitamin and mineral deficiencies. Sometimes, she was so weak and dizzy that she could not walk without falling. She struggled to eat well even when she had no appetite, and her friends and family helped. Her daughter did the grocery shopping for her, and her friends brought both meals and treats. She also learned to eat high-calorie foods, such as ice cream and cookies as often as possible. Sometimes, nothing tasted good, and she was just too nauseated to eat. Other times, she ate almost normally and concentrated on healthy foods. She was even able to make jokes about her situation. She kept a journal and during the chemotherapy treatment once wrote, "WOW. I am well over 35 pounds lighter and isn't that fantastic?! I know what you are thinking, what a way to lose it though, am I right?! Yes, it wasn't

For people undergoing treatment for colon cancer, getting proper nutrition, staying active, and coping with fatigue are serious challenges. Nutrition is an especially important part of cancer treatment.

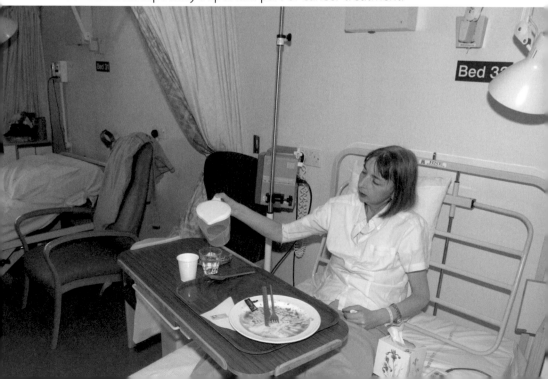

my preferred way to go but hey it's not like I'm not eating!! I'm eating plenty of healthy things and even a few cookies along the way, too! Just plenty of water to wash it all down, instead of Mountain Dew. Darn it all."[46]

Today, Kritz has completed her cancer treatment and is healthy once again. She is fifty years old and celebrating two years of being cancer free and in remission. She says, "It is time to move on, time to move forward and to Celebrate LIFE!"[47] She has recovered from all the side effects of her cancer treatment. Her fatigue is gone, and she is able to lead an active life. Her hair, which fell out during chemotherapy, has grown back, and she just needs checkups every six months to ensure that she stays healthy. She feels good about herself and is happy to have put the difficult side effects of treatment behind her.

Moving Forward

Sometimes, however, it is not so easy to overcome the effects of cancer treatment, especially when people feel permanently changed. Problems such as hair loss during chemotherapy are temporary. Hair grows back once treatment is ended, but, says the American Cancer Society, more permanent results of cancer, such as ostomies, alter one's physical appearance and can affect a person's self-image. People can feel sad and depressed about their altered appearance or even feel less worthwhile than they did before the cancer struck. Darrick Price, for example, had to adjust to a permanent alteration of his body when he was sixteen years old. The tumor was in the lower part of his colon, and even though his surgeon was able to remove it, the tumor had already grown large enough to have destroyed the muscle near his rectum. Because of the damage, Price needed a permanent colostomy. At first, he had a hard time accepting the change to his body. He remembers, "Because of this, my only real concern after surgery was if I would ever find a woman who would love me with this condition and who would also want children with me." It took some time, but as the years passed, Price learned that his colostomy did not really matter. He says, "Some women care and others don't."[48] Eighteen years after his surgery, he is living a fulfilling, cancer-free life and no longer worries about his physical differences.

Though all patients experience colon cancer and life after treatment differently, almost all colon cancer survivors agree with Price about one thing: They want to see colon cancer diagnosed early so that others do not have to go through the same struggles. Price urges people to protect their health by getting regular checkups for colon cancer. The Colon Cancer Alliance has an even larger goal. Its vision for the future is "eliminating the suffering and death caused by colorectal cancer."[49] New discoveries and emerging treatments are helping to make that goal a reality.

CHAPTER FIVE

The Future of Colon Cancer

The Colon Cancer Alliance, the American Cancer Society, the National Cancer Institute, and many other organizations share some of the same goals when it comes to colon cancer. They want to be able to prevent the disease. They want to identify and understand the cause or causes of colon cancer. They want a future in which all people with colon cancer can be treated and successfully cured. Although these goals may be difficult to achieve, they are not impossible. Researchers say they are making rapid progress toward unraveling the mysteries of colon cancer.

Screenings and Saved Lives

The prevention of colon cancer is an achievable goal, say researchers, and one that could be successfully attained in the near future. According to the American Cancer Society, more than 80 percent of cases of colorectal cancer could be prevented with universal annual screening programs (such as colonoscopies). Today, however, only about 50 percent of the people who should be screened are actually receiving checkups. In 2011 journalist Katie Couric partnered with the American Cancer Society to launch a public health educational campaign to persuade people that cancer screening saves lives. Couric is especially dedicated to colon cancer prevention

Journalist Katie Couric, who lost her husband to colon cancer, partnered with the American Cancer Society in 2011 to launch a public health education campaign to persuade people to get a colon cancer screening.

because her husband died of colon cancer in 1998. Since that time, she has been an advocate of early colon cancer screening for all people over the age of fifty and younger people with colon cancer in their families. In 2000 she established the National Colorectal Cancer Research Alliance (NCCRA), an organization with the goal of ending the threat of colon cancer through research funding and prevention education. She says today, "We have been able to accomplish a lot . . . since we established the NCCRA, but we still have miles to go in terms of awareness. Many people still aren't aware that there are screening procedures that can save lives."[50]

Thomas Frieden, director of the Centers for Disease Control and Prevention (CDC), agrees with Couric that education about screening for colon cancer is an ongoing need. He himself had a colonoscopy when he turned fifty in 2011 in which his doctor found and removed four polyps. He publicly announced the results of his colonoscopy in order to persuade other people to understand the importance of colon cancer screening. He says, "Now I anticipate that I will never have colon cancer because I will continue to have follow-ups to ensure that if there are growths, they're removed before they become cancerous." He adds that persuading the public to accept screening is not the only problem. Doctors have to be educated, too, if cases of colon cancer are to be prevented in the future. Frieden explains that today, the "largest single risk factor for not being screened for colorectal cancer is someone's doctor not recommending that they be screened."[51] Because of advocates such as Couric and Frieden, the CDC says that sixteen thousand colorectal cancer deaths have been prevented since 2003, but the CDC wants to do more. Its goal is to ensure that at least 70.5 percent of people who should be screened are screened by the year 2020. If that target goal is met, says the CDC, an additional one thousand colorectal deaths will be prevented each year in the United States. By preventing colon cancer or catching it early through widespread screening efforts, the National Cancer Institute predicts that a 50 percent reduction in colorectal cancer deaths is possible by 2020.

Mapping the Cancer Genome

Screening everyone for polyps is one critical way to prevent colon cancer deaths, but prevention and successful treatment also might be accomplished by understanding the genetic causes of colon cancer. To explore the genetics of cancer, the National Institutes of Health and the National Cancer Institute have established a research program called The Cancer Genome Atlas (TCGA). An individual's genome is his or her complete set of DNA. The DNA in an individual's thousands of genes provides the instructions that direct how each cell functions. Other parts of the genome act to turn genes on and off. This means that the genes in each cell are turned on according to the specific work that the cell has to do. For example, in a muscle cell, only the genes that make muscle proteins are functioning, while the genes that are needed to make liver proteins are turned off in that cell. Proteins do the work of the cell. Most genes and DNA are the same for everyone, but each individual's complete genome is slightly different. Scientists say that slight changes, or mutations—somewhat like typographical errors—in an individual's DNA can result

A genetic map of the human chromosome 17 is arranged in a circle. The colored bands represent genes (green), cancer genes (red) and other disease genes (orange).

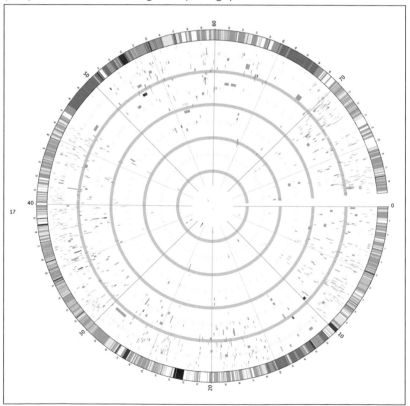

in a cell that does not function normally. "In cancer," explains TCGA, "these changes cause cells to survive and grow out of control, causing damage to surrounding tissues."[52] In other words, the wrong amount of a protein or an incorrectly made protein leads to a malfunctioning cell that, because of faulty DNA instructions, is not turned off. Researchers with TCGA are trying to find the genomic changes that result in more than twenty different kinds of cancer.

To identify the genomic changes that lead to cancer, researchers around the world collect tissue samples from people with cancer who agree to participate in the project. Then the researchers analyze the samples by comparing the DNA in normal tissue with the DNA in cancer tissue, looking for the slight coding differences that caused the cancer to grow. They compare the DNA of cancer tissues across many individuals to identify how the cancer cells may differ from one another. Finally, TCGA is creating a map, or an atlas, of all the genomic changes for all the kinds of cancer the researchers are studying. In the future, says TCGA, researchers will be able to utilize the atlas to personalize cancer care—to treat each person's cancer according to the exact genetic change that caused it to arise.

TCGA researchers have years to go before they complete their atlas. TCGA explains, "Finding the changes in the genome responsible for a cancer is like finding a needle in a haystack."[53] For colorectal cancer, the necessary tissues have been collected from volunteers, and, says TCGA, they are in the pipeline for DNA analysis. When the analysis is complete, TCGA researchers hope to discover how specific genetic changes determine whether the tumor responds to chemotherapy and radiation treatment, whether the DNA errors are different depending on where in the colon or rectum the tumor grows, and how colon cancer and rectal cancer are similar or different on the genetic level.

What Treatment for Which Mutation?

One way that knowledge of genetic changes and mutations can be used involves making treatment decisions. In 2008 and 2010, for example, two research studies examined treatment success for people with colon cancer that is associated with certain mutations in a gene known as the KRAS gene. The researchers compared people with mutated KRAS genes to people with normal KRAS genes. All the patients were treated with the targeted therapy drug cetuximab. For people with normal KRAS genes, the drug seemed effective. Other participants had several different mutations in the KRAS gene. For those with one particular mutation in the gene, cetuximab was also effective. For those with other KRAS mutations, the drug did not work; these people went through the treatment for nothing. One of the leaders of the research, Derek Jonker, says, "These results represent an exciting transition in the treatment of cancer. Whereas in the past . . . we treated a large number of people and had a small effect, we now begin to have the ability to identify the patients who are most likely to benefit and then tailor treatment based on the unique genetic makeup of each person's cancer."[54]

The National Cancer Institute says that studies such as those with the KRAS genes are evidence that colon cancer patients should undergo genetic testing before they begin treatment in order to be sure that people receive treatment that works for them. So far, scientists cannot identify all the genes that should be tested, but someday they hope to be able to identify the drugs that will work for each genetic mutation.

Harnessing Anticancer Genes

In the future, another way to tackle colon cancer gene mutations might be by turning on, or triggering, anticancer genes. In 2010 a research team at the University of Copenhagen in Denmark identified a gene called CDX2 that controls more than six hundred other genes that provide the instructions for proper functioning of the layer of cells that line the colon. The CDX2 gene "tells" a cell that it is in the epithelium of the colon and thus ensures that its genes function correctly—they instruct epithelial cells to do their jobs and not grow out of control. The researchers explain that CDX2 could be considered an

A Vaccine for Colon Cancer

A vaccine is a substance that uses the body's immune system to prevent disease. The immune system is the body's complex way of defending itself from foreign invaders, such as germs. To destroy an invader, immune system factors called B cells produce a type of protein called antibodies that latch onto the proteins on the surface of an invader cell and chemically mark it as being foreign to the body. Then other immune system cells destroy the invader. Cancer is not caused by germs, but cancer cells do have abnormal proteins on their surfaces. Cancer cells suppress the immune system so that it does not destroy them, but some researchers are trying to change that. Researcher Olivera Finn and her team at the University of Pittsburgh have developed a vaccine that is made of antibodies to a protein called MUC1 that is common on colorectal cancer tumor cells but not on normal cells. They are testing the vaccine in people with precancerous polyps to see if the vaccine's antibodies can prevent cancer. The trial is still ongoing, but Finn hopes that her vaccine will trigger an immune system response that destroys the abnormal cells before they become cancerous in people at high risk for the disease.

Vaccines are being developed for some cancers, including colon cancer. A team at the University of Pittsburgh recently developed a vaccine made of antibodies to a protein called MUC1 that is common on colorectal cancer tumor cells.

identity gene. One of the scientists, Jesper Troelsen, says, "We have also studied early stages of colon cancer. We observed that before the colonic cancer cells began to invade the tissue outside the colon, they deactivated the CDX2 gene, removing their 'ID.'"[55] Since cancer cells are not normal colon cells, an activated CDX2 gene would be an anticancer gene and would be the key to stopping the progression of cancer. It would tell a cancer cell to be a colon lining cell and function normally. How and why cancer cells deactivate CDX2 and how to prevent the deactivation is still unknown today. Troelsen and his colleagues are continuing to study how cancer cells deactivate the CDX2 gene and are trying to discover how to reactivate it. If they succeed, they will have found a genetic method of halting the growth of cancer cells in the colon.

The "Guardian of the Genome"

Another approach to treating cancer at the genetic level involves infecting a cancer cell with a virus. In about half of all cancers, including colon cancer, one genetic mutation is in the gene that carries the instructions for making the protein called p53. p53 is an important protein because it prevents a cell with damaged DNA from multiplying and growing until the DNA damage can be repaired. If the damage cannot be repaired, p53 signals the cell to destroy itself. A cell that lacks p53 grows and multiplies no matter how damaged it is. Cancer is the uncontrolled growth of cells, so a mutation in the gene that codes for p53 is, at least in part, a hallmark of a cancer cell. British cancer specialist and oncologist David P. Lane discovered the p53 gene in 1979 and considers the gene to be the "guardian of the genome."[56] Ever since Lane's discovery, he and other scientists have been working to develop therapies that take advantage of this characteristic of cancer cells. They try to replace the missing p53 gene or develop medicines that attack cells without p53.

In one treatment method, scientists use an adenovirus—a common virus that causes respiratory infections—that has been made harmless in a laboratory. A normal p53 gene is added to the virus, and it is directly injected into the tumor so that the cancer cells will be infected with the virus. Despite being harmless or deactivated, the virus still acts like a normal virus, slipping inside the cell and forcing it to substitute the

Computer artwork of the tumor suppressor protein p53, left, bound to a molecule of DNA. The protein binds to specific sequences in the DNA and halts cell replication.

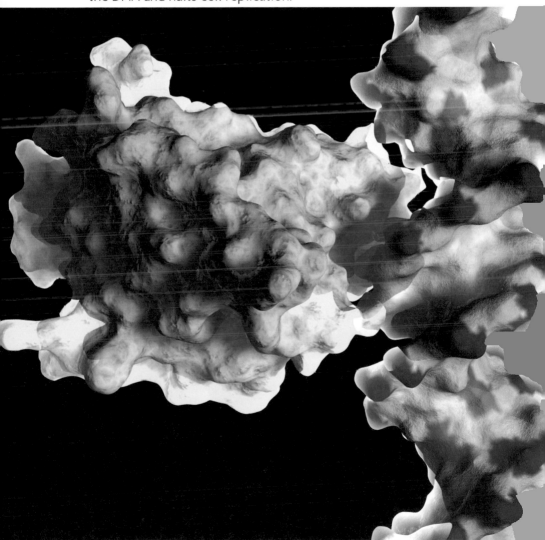

Colorectal Cancer and Vitamin D

Vitamin D, which is absorbed through the skin during exposure to sunlight and is found in some foods, has been associated with improved immune system functioning and increased resistance to diseases, and some studies provide evidence that high blood levels of vitamin D can lower the risk of colorectal cancer. In laboratory dishes, scientists have found that vitamin D slows the growth of cancer cells and promotes apoptosis. One large study of more than 500,000 people in Europe reported in 2010 that people with the highest vitamin D levels in their blood had 40 percent less risk of developing colon cancer than people with the lowest levels. Other studies have found that people being treated for colon cancer are less likely to die of the disease if their vitamin D blood levels are high. The National Cancer Institute, however, is not ready to recommend that people take vitamin D supplements to prevent or treat colorectal cancer. This is because not all vitamin D research studies have found the same results. More research is needed, but many scientists today are impressed by the growing evidence that vitamin D may help people fight colon cancer.

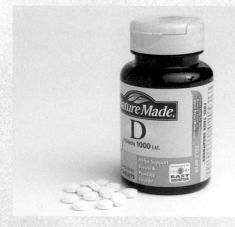

A 2010 study of 500,000 people in Europe reported that people with the highest levels of vitamin D in their blood were 40 percent less likely to develop colon cancer than people with the lowest.

virus's genetic instructions for the cell's genetic instructions. The infection thus replaces the cell's missing or defective p53 with normal p53. Theoretically, this treatment would stop cancer growth and destroy cancer cells. In the laboratory and with animals, the treatment seems to work, but more research needs to be done with people. A major difficulty is ensuring that every cancer cell is infected, and this is especially difficult for tumors inside the colon. Another problem is that the patient's immune system eventually begins to fight off and kill the virus. A third problem is that p53 is suppressed not only by cancer cells but also from the stress that cancer can cause to other, normal cells.

Lane and other researchers around the world are working to develop powerful combination drugs, somewhat like in molecular targeted therapy, that target all cancer cells and do not harm normal cells. They are working with a chemical drug compound called Nutlin that activates p53 in all the body cells. Nutlin temporarily stops all the normal cells from being able to duplicate DNA. Cancer cells, however, with no p53, are unaffected. Then a second drug which targets and kills cells that are duplicating their DNA and dividing can be injected into the patient's body. Lane and his colleagues explain, "The second drug is designed to kill only proliferating cells and is thus able to now kill only the p53 mutant tumor cells but not the normal proliferating tissues."[57] After this treatment, when the cancer cells are killed, the effects of Nutlin can be reversed so that normal cells are unharmed and can resume normal functioning.

So far, combination drugs and gene therapy with Nutlin is still in the laboratory research stage, but researchers such as Lane are excited about the possibilities for future cancer treatment. One of Lane's colleagues, Chit Fang Cheok, explains, "One [of] the most difficult problems in treating cancer is ensuring that normal, healthy cells are not killed over the course of treatment. Many of the currently available methods of treatment, such as chemotherapy and radiation therapy, damage normal cells in the process of killing cancer cells. We are using our knowledge of p53 to overcome this difficulty."[58] Lane himself calls the research "potentially very positive and exciting."[59]

Old Treatments Used in New Ways

Someday, colon cancer may be treated and cured at the genetic level, and two scientists in Germany and the United States believe that they have found another drug that could help make this happen. In 2011 Ulrike Stein and Robert H. Shoemaker discovered that an old drug that has been used for sixty years to fight tapeworm infections in the intestines seems to stop colon cancer from metastasizing. The drug is called niclosamide. In laboratory dishes of cancer cells, the researchers found that niclosamide can suppress the activity of a mutant gene that triggers metastasis. When the researchers gave niclosamide to mice with cancer, they discovered that the mice had fewer metastases than mice that did not receive the drug. Now the two researchers are planning a clinical trial to see if the drug works the same way for people.

Another class of common drugs that may prevent colon cancer and polyps in vulnerable people is aspirin and other NSAIDs (non-steroidal anti-inflammatory drugs, such as Aleve, Advil, or Celebrex). Many studies have found that people who regularly use these drugs have a lower risk of developing colon cancer. In people with the genetic syndrome FAP, which leads to growth of polyps, the U.S. Food and Drug Administration (FDA) has approved Celebrex to prevent or reduce the frequency of recurring polyps. Clinical trials to assess the value of other NSAIDs for preventing colon cancer are still ongoing. Scientists have not yet determined whether they should be used by everyone to reduce the risk of colon cancer, but they may be able to make recommendations in just a few years.

Other treatments could come in the form of currently available mineral supplements. Polyps, for example, someday may be prevented from growing in the colon with a simple mineral supplement. Selenium is considered to be an essential trace mineral in the human diet. It is found in foods such as seafood, liver, and some grains, nuts, and seeds. Because previous trials and studies found that high levels of selenium in

Selenium, an essential trace mineral in the human diet, has been found to reduce the risk of polyp growth. Researchers are now conducting large-scale trials to determine the value of selenium in fighting cancer.

the blood reduce the risk of polyp growth, researchers at the University of Arizona are conducting a large-scale clinical trial to determine the value of selenium. About eighteen hundred volunteers who have already had a colon polyp removed are participating in the study. Half the volunteers will receive a daily selenium supplement; the other half will receive a fake pill, called a placebo. The trial is expected to last from three to five years, and at its end, the researchers will compare the number of people who have recurring polyps in each group. If polyps recur much less often in the selenium group than in the placebo group, the researchers will know that selenium is a good preventive treatment. They will know whether people who have had polyps in the past can prevent polyps and the risk of colon cancer by taking selenium.

Breakthroughs and Hope for the Future

Despite all the progress that is being made to understand, prevent, and treat colon cancer, the American Cancer Society points out that there is "still no magic bullet," and it is unlikely that there ever will be, because colon cancer is such a complex disease. The American Cancer Society explains, "With all of the mistakes that lead to a cell becoming cancerous, it is likely that scientists will need to use a number of different approaches in combination—including newer therapies and traditional surgery, chemotherapy, and radiation—to make a real impact on the course of cancer."[60] Making that impact, however, is the goal of researchers today. As of 2011 the National Institutes of Health listed nearly eight hundred ongoing studies of colon cancer at the Clinical Trials website. All of these studies are recruiting human volunteers with colon cancer in order to research new drugs or treatments or to understand the cause of the disease or to determine how to prevent it.

The Conquer Cancer Foundation of the American Society of Clinical Oncology is dedicated to the vision of "a world free from the fear of cancer." The organization, founded by cancer doctors, supports and funds cancer research and public education with the mission of making cancer a disease of the past. The foundation believes that a cancer-free future is possible. It says, "We dare to imagine it because we know that every day, with every breakthrough and every new treatment, we're one step closer to conquering cancer."[61] For people with colon cancer, the breakthroughs could mean that even stage IV cancer may become an easily treatable, curable disease.

Notes

Introduction: A Scary Disease

1. Hayley Storrs. "My Mother's Bowel Cancer Story." Tips on Coping Emotionally. Cancer Research UK. http://can cerhelp.cancerresearchuk.org/coping-with-cancer/tips /emotionally/my-mothers-bowel-cancer-story.
2. National Cancer Institute, NIH, DHHS. Introduction to *Cancer Trends Progress Report—2009/2010 Update.* Bethesda, MD: National Cancer Institute, April 2010. http://progressreport.cancer.gov.
3. Quoted in Women's Health.gov. "News: Interview with a Colon Cancer Survivor: Jen Puglise." February 1, 2011. www.womenshealth.gov/news/spotlight/2011/2.cfm.
4. Quoted in Tim Dickinson. "Docs: Herman Cain's Cancer Is Not Disqualifying." *Rolling Stone*, October 13, 2011. www.rollingstone.com/politics/blogs/national-affairs /docs-herman-cains-cancer-isnt-disqualifying-20111012.
5. Quoted in Dickinson. "Docs: Herman Cain's Cancer Is Not Disqualifying."

Chapter One: What Is Colon Cancer?

6. Quoted in End Colon Cancer Now.org. "Patient Story: Anita Mitchell." Fred Hutchinson Cancer Research Center. www.endcoloncancernow.org/about/stories.html.
7. National Cancer Institute. "What Is Cancer?" NCI Cancer Library. www.cancer.gov/cancertopics/cancerlibrary/what -is-cancer.
8. National Cancer Institute. "What Is Cancer?"
9. Bernard Levin, Terri Ades, Durado Brooks, Christopher H. Crane, Paulo M. Hoff, Paul J. Limburg, and David A. Rothenberger, eds. *American Cancer Society's Complete Guide to Colorectal Cancer.* Atlanta, GA: American Cancer Society, 2006, p. 7.

10. Levin et al. *American Cancer Society's Complete Guide to Colorectal Cancer*, p. 9.
11. Levin et al. *American Cancer Society's Complete Guide to Colorectal Cancer*, p.75.
12. Levin et al. *American Cancer Society's Complete Guide to Colorectal Cancer*, p. 79.
13. Colon Cancer Alliance. "Personal Stories: Heidi." http://cc alliance.org/stories/heidi.html.

Chapter Two: The Cause and Diagnosis of Colon Cancer

14. Molly McMaster. "Molly's Story." Rolling to Recovery. www.rollingtorecovery.com/story.htm.
15. Cancer Help UK. "What Is Cancer? How Cancer Starts." Cancer Research UK. http://cancerhelp.cancerresearchuk .org/about-cancer/what-is-cancer/cells/how-cancer-starts #genes_repair.
16. Mayo Clinic Staff. "Colon Cancer: Risk Factors," August 13, 2011. www.mayoclinic.com/health/colon-cancer/DS00 035/DSECTION=risk-factors.
17. Quoted in Zosia Chustecka. "Exercise Reduces Risk for Colon Polyps, Resulting in Less Colon Cancer." Medscape Medical News. Medscape, March 9, 2011. www.medscape .com/viewarticle/738649.
18. Mayo Clinic Staff. "Colon Cancer: Risk Factors."
19. Levin et al. *American Cancer Society's Complete Guide to Colorectal Cancer*, pp. 35–36.
20. Quoted in Centers for Disease Control and Prevention. "Colorectal (Colon) Cancer: Personal Screening Stories," January 27, 2011. www.cdc.gov/cancer/colorectal/basic _info/stories.htm.
21. Levin et al. *American Cancer Society's Complete Guide to Colorectal Cancer*, p. 64.

Chapter Three: Treatment of Colon Cancer

22. National Cancer Institute. "Colon Cancer Treatment (PDQ®)." National Institutes of Health, August 05, 2011, p.1. www.cancer.gov/cancertopics/pdq/treatment/colon /HealthProfessional/page1.

23. Quoted in Colon Cancer Alliance. "Personal Stories: Cynthia." http://ccalliance.org/stories/cynthia.html.

24. Darrick Price. "Embracing Life After Colon Cancer." Feature. *WebMD the Magazine*. www.webmd.com/colorectal-cancer/features/darrick-price-colon-cancer-survivor.

25. Levin et al. *American Cancer Society's Complete Guide to Colorectal Cancer*, p. 194.

26. Bowel Cancer Australia. "Real Life Stories: Brian's Story." http://bowelcanceraustralia.org/bca/index.php?option=com_content&view=article&id=483&catid=51&Itemid=489.

27. Mayo Clinic Staff, "Colon Cancer: Treatments and Drugs." Mayo Clinic, August 13, 2011. www.mayoclinic.com/health/colon-cancer/DS00035/DSECTION=treatments-and-drugs.

28. Quoted in Bowel Cancer Australia. "Real Life Stories: Gillian's Story," http://bowelcanceraustralia.org/bca/index.php?option=com_content&view=article&id=311&catid=51&Itemid=489.

29. CancerConnect.com. "Understanding Targeted Therapy for Colorectal Cancer." http://news.cancerconnect.com/colon-cancertipsunderstanding-targeted-therapy-for-colorectal-cancer/.

30. Mayo Clinic Staff. "Treatments and Drugs: Colon Cancer." Mayo Clinic, August 13, 2011. www.mayoclinic.com/health/colon-cancer/DS00035/DSECTION=treatments-and-drugs.

31. Levin et al. *American Cancer Society's Complete Guide to Colorectal Cancer*, p. 210.

32. Quoted in Cancer.Net. "John Peterson—Colon Cancer." Patient Stories: Narratives from Participants in Cancer Clinical Trials. American Society of Clinical Oncology, April 9, 2009. www.cancer.net/patient/All+About+Cancer/Clinical+Trials/Patient+Stories%3A+Narratives+from+Participants+in+Cancer+Clinical+Trials/John+Peterson+-+Colon+Cancer.

33. Quoted in Cancer.Net. "John Peterson—Colon Cancer."

Chapter Four: Living with Colon Cancer

34. Quoted in Alice Park. "How to Handle a Medical Crisis." Q&A with Jessie Gruman. *Time Health*, July 11, 2007. www.time.com/time/health/article/0,8599,1642253-1,00.html.

35. Jessie Gruman. "When the Diagnosis Is Scary." *Parade Magazine*, 2007. www.parade.com/articles/editions/2007 /edition_01-14-2007/Diagnosis.
36. Quoted in Park. "How to Handle a Medical Crisis."
37. Levin et al. *American Cancer Society's Complete Guide to Colorectal Cancer*, p. 104.
38. Fredenishen_r. "Colon Cancer Stage 4 Survival Stories." eHealth Forum, July 7, 2007. http://ehealthforum.com /health/topic99429.html.
39. Quoted in Ellen Crean. "A Life Saver, in His Fashion." CBS News, February 11, 2009. www.cbsnews.com/stories /2006/07/14/earlyshow/saturday/main1806164.shtml.
40. Quoted in American Cancer Society. "Survivor Learns to Live with Colon Cancer." Stories of Hope. American Cancer Society, September 28, 2011. www.cancer.org/Treatment /SurvivorshipDuringandAfterTreatment/StoriesofHope /survivor-learns-to-live-with-colon-cancer.
41. Quoted in Colon Cancer Alliance. "Personal Stories: Claudia." www.ccalliance.org/stories/claudia.html.
42. Quoted in American Cancer Society. "Stories of Hope: Colon Cancer Builds a Character," November 18, 2005. www.cancer.org/Treatment/SurvivorshipDuringandAfter Treatment/StoriesofHope/colon-cancer-builds-a-character.
43. Quoted in American Cancer Society. "Stories of Hope: Kathy Croswell's Story," May 1, 2001. www.cancer.org /Treatment/SurvivorshipDuringandAfterTreatment/Stories ofHope/kathycroswellsstory.
44. American Cancer Society. "Treatment: Nutrition for the Person with Cancer During Treatment: A Guide for Patients and Families," August 2, 2010. www.cancer.org /Treatment/SurvivorshipDuringandAfterTreatment/Nutri tionforPeoplewithCancer/NutritionforthePersonwith Cancer/nutrition-during-treatment-intro.
45. Get Your Rear in Gear. "Survivor Stories: Becky Kritz." http://getyourrearingear.com/stories/survivor-stories /becky-kritz.
46. Becky Kritz. "Tuesday, July 8, 2008 4:45 PM CDT, Becky Kritz: Journal." CaringBridge.org. www.caringbridge.org /visit/beckykritz/journal/11/createdAt/asc.

47. Becky Kritz. "Journal: Thursday, September 16, 2010 9:52 PM CDT." CaringBridge.org. www.caringbridge.org/visit /beckykritz.

48. Price. "Embracing Life After Colon Cancer."

49. Colon Cancer Alliance. "About Us: Mission & Vision." www.ccalliance.org/about/mission.html.

Chapter Five: The Future of Colon Cancer

50. Quoted in PR Newswire. "American Cancer Society and Katie Couric Partner with Media Planet to Publish One of the Largest Cancer Awareness Campaigns in US History." United Business Media, September 24, 2011. www.prnews wire.com/news-releases/american-cancer-society-and-katie -couric-partner-with-mediaplanet-to-publish-one-of-the -largest-cancer-awareness-campaigns-in-us-history-10371 5214.html.

51. Quoted in Richard Knox. "Colorectal Cancer Deaths Declining, but Millions Still Aren't Getting Screened." NPR, July 5, 2011. www.npr.org/blogs/health/2011/07/05/137633255 /colorectal-cancer-deaths-declining-but-millions-still-arent -getting-screened.

52. The Cancer Genome Atlas. "Cancer Genomics: What Does It Mean for You?" NIH Publication No. 10-7556, July, 2010. http://cancergenome.nih.gov/PublishedContent /Files/pdfs/1.1.0_CancerGenomics_TCGA-Genomics-Bro chure-508.pdf.

53. The Cancer Genome Atlas. "Cancer Genomics."

54. Quoted in NCI Cancer Bulletin. "Colorectal Cancer Trials Support Gene Testing for Two Drugs." Clinical Trial Results. National Cancer Institute, 2010. www.cancer.gov /clinicaltrials/results/summary/2008/genetest1108.

55. Quoted in Science Daily. "Stopping Colon Cancer by Activating Anti-Cancer Genes," August 31, 2010. www .sciencedaily.com/releases/2010/08/100830114949.htm.

56. Quoted in A*STAR. "Biography: Professor Sir David Lane." Agency for Science, Technology, and Research, Singapore, November 13, 2009. www.a-star.edu.sg/About ASTAR/CorporateProfile/SeniorManagement/ProfSir DavidLane/tabid/294/Default.aspx.

57. David P. Lane, Chit Fang Cheok, and Sonia Lain. "P53-Based Cancer Therapy." *Cold Spring Harbor Perspectives in Biology.* Vol. 2: a001222, May 12, 2010, p. 6. http://csh perspectives.cshlp.org/content/2/9/a001222.full.

58. Quoted in Insciences Organisation. "Singapore Scientists Exploit Knowledge of p53 for a Novel Way of Increasing Specificity of Cancer Treatments," May 21, 2010. http://in sciences.org/article.php?article_id=9013.

59. David P. Lane. "Interview with Sir David P. Lane, Ph.D." Frontiers in Basic Cancer Research. American Association for Cancer Research, September 14, 2011. www.aacr .org/home/public--media/multimedia-/aacr-podcasts/2011 -frontiers-in-basic-cancer-research podcasts-/interview-with -sir-david-p-lane,-phd.aspx.

60. Levin et al *American Cancer Society's Complete Guide to Colorectal Cancer*, p. 220.

61. Conquer Cancer Foundation. "Conquer Cancer Foundation Overview," American Society of Clinical Oncologists. www.conquercancerfoundation.org/foundation/Who %20We%20Are/Our%20Story/Foundation%20Information /Mission,%20Vision,%20Case%20Statement/CCF_Found ation_Overview.pdf.

Glossary

adenoma: A tumor that develops in the epithelial tissue, or inner lining, of certain organs.

anastomosis: A surgical procedure in which the two healthy sections of the colon or rectum are connected after the cancerous portion has been removed.

apoptosis: Programmed cell death.

benign: Not malignant or cancerous. A benign tumor does not invade other tissues, does not spread to other parts of the body, and does not usually threaten health or life.

carcinogen: Any substance capable of causing cancer.

chemotherapy: Treatment of cancer with drugs that kill cancer cells.

clinical trial: Controlled research with a new medical treatment to evaluate its safety and possible benefits in people. In the United States, clinical trials must be conducted under the direction of the Food and Drug Administration before a new drug or treatment can be approved for general use.

colonoscopy: A medical procedure for examining the inside of the colon and rectum.

DNA (deoxyribonucleic acid): The chemicals in genes that carry the coding instructions for body structures and functions.

epithelium: The thin lining of tissue on the inside surfaces of the gastrointestinal tract.

gastrointestinal tract: The digestive system; basically the long tube that begins at the mouth and ends at the anus and includes the stomach and intestines.

gene: A discrete segment of DNA on a specific point of a chromosome that carries a piece of specific hereditary information for making proteins and for determining how cells function.

genome: The complete set of genetic material in a living thing.

malignant: Having the properties of invasiveness and metastasis.

metastasis: Transmission, or spreading, of cancerous cells from the original site to one or more other sites in the body, usually through the blood system or the lymph system. The plural is metastases. The secondary tumor, growing in the new site, is referred to as a metastasis. When a cancer has spread, it is said to have metastasized.

mutation: An alteration, variation, or a change in the DNA structure of a gene that is permanent and can be passed on to offspring.

ostomy: A surgical procedure that creates an artificial opening for the elimination of body wastes. A colostomy involves bringing one end of the cut colon to the opening in the abdomen, while in an ileostomy the end of the ileum is brought to the opening.

polyp: A growth or mass of tissue protruding from the lining of a body organ.

proliferate: Grow or multiply by rapidly producing new cells.

radiation therapy: The use of high-energy rays (such as X-rays) to damage and destroy cancer cells.

recurrence: Happening or returning again. The return or reappearance of cancer cells after some time (months or years) with no disease.

resection: Surgical removal of the diseased part of an organ.

screening test: A medical test performed when no disease symptoms are evident in order to check for disease or conditions that could lead to disease.

staging: A medical description of the extent or severity of a cancer. The cancer staging system describes the location, size, and spread of the disease.

stoma: An artificial opening in the abdomen where part of the intestine protrudes. A stoma is formed during an ostomy.

targeted therapy: Chemical treatment that specifically targets the key molecules responsible for cancer growth but does not target normal cells. Also known as molecularly targeted therapy.

tumor: A swelling in any part of the body caused by the abnormal growth of tissue. Tumors may be malignant, but most are benign.

Organizations to Contact

American Cancer Society

250 Williams St. NW
Atlanta, GA 30303
Phone: (800) 227-2345
Website: www.cancer.org

Anyone touched by any kind of cancer may contact the American Cancer Society at any time for information and support.

Colon Cancer Alliance

175 Ninth Ave.
New York, NY 10011
Phone: (877) 422-2030
Website: www.ccalliance.org

The Colon Cancer Alliance offers education, advocacy, and support for people affected by colon cancer. Its many services include a telephone helpline and an online buddy program.

Fight Colorectal Cancer

1414 Prince St., Suite 204
Alexandria, VA 22314
Phone: (877) 427-2111
E-mail: info@fightcolorectalcancer.org
Website: http://fightcolorectalcancer.org

This is an organization that trains citizen advocates, empowers survivors to fight for improved treatment and research for colorectal cancer, and educates government lawmakers about the policies needed to fight cancer. It also offers patient and family support through its toll-free "answer line" and online.

National Cancer Institute (NCI)

NCI Public Inquiries Office
Bldg. 31, Room 10A03
Bethesda, MD 20892-2580
Phone: (800) 422-6237
Website: www.cancer.gov

This is an agency of the U.S. government that provides extensive educational information about cancer to both the general public and health professionals. It also provides the latest information about ongoing clinical trials.

United Ostomy Associations of America (UOAA)

PO Box 512
Northfield, MN 55057-0512
Phone: (800) 826-0826
E-mail: info@ostomy.org
Website: www.ostomy.org

The UOAA is a national organization dedicated to providing advocacy, information, and support to people with ostomies and their families. It offers a magazine, online discussion forums, and a telephone helpline.

For More Information

Books

Donna Bozzone. *Cancer Genetics*. New York: Chelsea House, 2007. The author explains genetic mutations as they relate to cancer, oncogenes (genes that can lead to cancer), cancer suppressor genes, and how current knowledge of cancer genetics can result in new treatments and prevention of cancer.

Brenda Elsagher. *I'd Like to Buy a Bowel, Please*. Andover, MN: Expert Publishing, 2006. Although written for adults, this book is short and easy to read. It offers a humorous look at adjusting to life with an ostomy and provides stories from health professionals and patients themselves about real experiences and how to cope with the daily challenges.

Luke Graham. *It's Cancer. Now What?* New York: Rosen, 2011. This book discusses the diagnosis of cancer from a teen perspective. The author is honest about the fear of a cancer diagnosis and the challenges of treatment while offering up-to-date information about treatments, therapies, and prevention and answering questions about coping with cancer as a patient or a loved one.

Kara Rogers, ed. *The Digestive System*. New York: Rosen, 2010. This book explains in detail the processes involved in human digestion, the use of nutrients, and elimination of wastes, as well as what happens when something goes wrong in the digestive tract and the diseases and disorders that can result.

Websites

All About Cancer: Cancer Research UK (http://info.cancer researchuk.org/cancerandresearch/all-about-cancer). At this site from the organization Cancer Research UK, visitors can click the link for "why cancer starts" to see two animations that explain how healthy cells are made in the body and how cancer cells grow out of control.

ASGE Colonoscopy Video (www.asge.org/education-videos /colonvideo1.html). This video from the American Society for Gastrointestinal Endoscopy describes a colonoscopy procedure in detail.

CDC Vital Signs: Colorectal Cancer (www.cdc.gov/vital signs/cancerscreening). The Centers for Disease Control and Prevention (CDC) established Vital Signs to highlight important public health issues. At this site, the CDC provides data about the need for screening for colorectal cancer, along with graphs and maps that track the increased risk and decreased incidences of colon cancer.

Mayo Clinic: Colonoscopy (www.mayoclinic.com/health /colonoscopy/MM00010). The Mayo Clinic provides a short video of a polyp being removed from the colon lining during a colonoscopy.

Rolling to Recovery (www.rollingtorecovery.com/index.html). Cancer survivor Molly McMaster established this site to raise awareness among young people about the risks of colon cancer and the need for screening, as well as to tell her own story about her struggle with colon cancer.

Index

A

Adenomas, 15, 17, 30
Age
   incidence of colon cancer
      by, 21, *21*
   as risk factor for colon
      cancer, 28
Alcohol use, 29
American Cancer Society,
   17, 63, 64, 65, 69
   on alternative treatments,
      53
   on cancer grading, 18
   on cancer screening, 31
   on chemotherapy, 44
   on clinical trials, 50
   on coping with diagnosis,
      57, 61
   on imaging tests, 37
   on need for combination
      treatments, 82
   tumor staging system of,
      19–20
American Joint Committee
   on Cancer, 19
American Society of
   Clinical Oncology, 82
Anastomosis, 40, 41, *43*
Anus, 14
Apoptosis, 9–10
Aspirin, 80

B

Bevacizumab, 49
Biopsy, 38

C

Cain, Herman, 7
Cancer
   biology of, 9–12
   decline in new cases of/
      deaths from, 6
   grading of, 18
   staging of, 18–20
Cancer Genome Atlas
   (TCGA), 71, 73
Cancer Research UK, 26
Cancer Survivors Network
   (American Cancer
   Society), 63
Carcinoembryonic antigen
   (CEA), 36
Carcinogens, 29
Carcinomas, 12
CDX2 gene, 74, 76
CEA (carcinoembryonic
   antigen), 36
Cecum, 14
Celebrex, 80
Cells, 9–10
Centers for Disease
   Control and Prevention
   (CDC), 36, 71

Cetuximab, 49, 74
Chemotherapy, 44–46
   side effects of, 60, *62*,
      62–63
Chromosome(s), 9, *11*
   17, genetic map of, 72
Clinical trials, 50, 52, 82
Colectomy, 39–40
Colon, 12
   structures of, 14
Colon Cancer Alliance, 68
Colon cancer/colorectal
   cancer, *10*
   age-adjusted SEER
      incidence rates of, *21*
   diagnosis of, 35–38
   ethnicity and, 36–37
   genetics and, 26, 28
   grading of, 18
   percentage beginning as
      adenomas, 17
   sites of development of,
      15
   spread of, 17–18
   stages of, *19*, 20
   staging of, 18–20, 36–38
   survival rate for, 22–23
   symptoms of, 8, 16, 17
   See also Risk factors;
      Treatment(s)
Colonoscopy, 31–33, *32*,
   39
Colostomy, 41–44
Computerized tomographic
   colonography (CTC), 34
Computerized tomography
   (CT) scan, 37

Conquer Cancer
   Foundation (American
   Society of Clinical
   Oncology), 82–83
Couric, Katie, 69–71, *70*
CT (computerized
   tomography) scan, 37
CTC (computerized
   tomographic
   colonography), 34

D
Deaths/death rates,
   colorectal cancer, 6, 20
Deoxyribonucleic acid
   (DNA), 9, 71–72
   mutations in, 10–11, 25,
      72–73
   p53 tumor suppressor
      protein bound to, *77*
Diagnosis, 35–38
   coping with, 57–59
Diet/nutrition, 29, 64, 66
DNA. *See*
   Deoxyribonucleic acid

E
Electromagnetic therapy,
   53, *53*
Epithelium, 14
Exercise, 30, 61

F
Familial adenomatous
   polyposis (FAP), 28, 80
5-FU (5-fluorouracil), 46,
   48

G

Gastrointestinal (GI) tract,
12, *13*, 14
inflammation in, 30
Genes, 9, 11
CDX2, 74, 76
on chromosome 17, *72*
HNPCC, 26
KRAS, 74
p53, 76–77, 79–80
Genetics
of cancer, 9–12, 25–26
of colon cancer, 26, 28
in making treatment
choices, 73–74
Genome, 71–72
GI tract. *See*
Gastrointestinal tract

H

HNPCC gene, 26

I

Ileostomy, 41, 42, 43
Immune system, 11, 17
Insulin, 30

J

J-pouch surgery, 42, *43*

K

KRAS gene, 74

L

Lymph nodes, 17, 18
in cancer staging, 20
enlarged, 36

removal of, 41
sampling of, 38
Lymphatic system, 17–18

M

Magnetic resonance
imaging (MRI), 37–38
Mayo Clinic, 28, 31, 46,
49–50
Metabolic therapies, 53
Metastasis, 17–18
Microspheres, drug
delivery, *51*, 52
MRI (magnetic resonance
imaging), 37–38
Mucosa, 14
Muscularis propria, 14
Mutations, 10–11, 24, 72–73

N

National Cancer Institute
(National Institutes of
Health), 6, 9, 82
Cancer Genome Atlas
program of, 71, 73
on decline in colon
cancer death rates, 20
on genetic testing before
treatment, 74
on incidence of
colorectal cancer, 21
on symptoms of colon
cancer, 16
on treatability of colon
cancer, 39
on vitamin D for
prevention, 78

National Colorectal Cancer Research Alliance (NCCRA), 70
National Institutes of Health (NIH), 71, 82
NCCRA (National Colorectal Cancer Research Alliance), 70
Niclosamide, 80
Nonsteroidal anti-inflammatory drugs (NSAIDs), 80
Nutlin, 79
Nutrition/diet, 29, 64, 66

O
Oncogenes, *25*, 26
Ostomies, 41–44
coping with, 67–68
Oz, Mehmet, 27, *27*

P
p53 tumor suppressor gene/protein, 76–77, *77*, 79
Panitumumab, 49
Polypectomy, 39
Polyps, 15
cancerous, *15*
exercise and, 30
removal of, 32–33
removal surgery, *40*
screening for, 30–31
selenium and reduced risk of, 81–82
Positron emission tomography (PET), 38

R
Race/ethnicity, 36
colorectal cancer rates by, *37*
Radiation therapy, 46–48, *47*
Rectum, 14
digital examination of, 36
Recurrence, 22
Remission, 22
Resection and anastomosis, 40, 41
Risk factors, 24
age, 21
environmental/lifestyle, 29–30
genetic, 25, 28
for polyp development, 30

S
Screening
for colorectal cancer/polyps, 31
percent of at-risk people receiving, 69
potential reduction in colon cancer from, 71
Selective Internal Radiation Therapy (SIRT), 52, 54
Selenium, *81*, 81–82
Serosa, 14
Sigmoid colon, 14
Sigmoidoscopy, 33–34, *34*
SIRT (Selective Internal Radiation Therapy), 52, 54
Support groups, 63

Surgery, 39–44
  coping with, 67–68
  J-pouch surgery, 42, *43*
  polyp-removal, *40*
Symptoms, 8, 16, 17

T
Targeted therapy, 48–50
TCGA (Cancer Genome
  Atlas), 71, 73
TNM system, 19–20
Tobacco smoking, 29
Treatment(s), 8–9
  alternative, 53
  chemotherapy, 44–46

coping with, 59–60
experimental, 50, 52
radiation therapy, 46–48,
  47
surgical, 39–44
targeted therapy, 48–50
using established drugs,
  80–82
Tumor suppressor genes,
  27
Tumors, 10, 12

V
Vaccines, 75
Vitamin D, 78, *78*

Picture Credits

About the Author

Toney Allman holds a BS from Ohio State University and an MA from the University of Hawaii. She currently lives in Virginia and has written more than thirty nonfiction books for students on a variety of medical and scientific topics.